Simone Weil's
The Iliad *or the Poem of Force*

"Holoka deserves our gratitude for having provided this exemplary edition, which supplies all the help necessary for the non-classical reader to understand and appreciate the essay, but which also contains much that is of interest to the classicist.... All scholars interested in Homer, and all libraries of universities where literature is taught, should buy this book."

Richard Whitaker, University of Cape Town,
Scholia Reviews 13 (2004) 10

"Holoka's new presentation of Weil's essay as a text to be studied rather than an oracular utterance gives the essay an ongoing currency that it certainly deserves and helps us to appreciate it for what it is: a shaft of light illuminating one aspect of a complicated poem and an inspiring example of how an ancient Greek text can serve a modern reader struggling with her own life and times."

Sheila Murnaghan, University of Pennsylvania,
Bryn Mawr Classical Review 2004.02.24

"With Holoka's commentary at hand, we find that we are not merely reading Weil: we are seeing how Weil's interpretation of the *Iliad* may be situated in the context of scholarly works on Homer and in the context of meditations on war in general."

Rebecca Resinski, Hendrix College,
The Key Reporter [Phi Beta Kappa] 69.2 (Spring 2004) 11

"[Holoka's] sensitivity, not only to [Weil's] approach to the poem, but also to her direct and unelaborate style, is reflected in his translation, which is strong and simple, conveying the tragic weight of the original.... A welcome addition to Simone Weil studies, and one which brings out the relevance of the philosopher to today's war-torn world."

J.P. Little, St. Patrick's University College, Dublin,
French Studies 58.3 (2004) 438

S IMONE W EIL ' S
THE ILIAD *OR THE*
POEM OF FORCE

PETER LANG
New York • Washington, D.C./Baltimore • Bern
Frankfurt am Main • Berlin • Brussels • Vienna • Oxford

SIMONE WEIL'S
THE ILIAD OR THE POEM OF FORCE

A Critical Edition

JAMES P. HOLOKA
editor & translator

PETER LANG
New York • Washington, D.C./Baltimore • Bern
Frankfurt am Main • Berlin • Brussels • Vienna • Oxford

Library of Congress Cataloging-in-Publication Data

Weil, Simone.
Simone Weil's The Iliad or the poem of force : a critical edition /
edited and translated by James P. Holoka.
p. cm.
Includes bibliographical references and index.
1. Homer. Iliad. 2. Epic poetry, Greek—History and criticism.
3. Achilles (Greek mythology) in literature. 4. Trojan War—
Literature and the war. 5. Violence in literature.
I. Holoka, James P. II. Title.
PA4037 .W35   883'.01—dc21   2002152524
ISBN 978-0-8204-6361-2

Die Deutsche Bibliothek-CIP-Einheitsaufnahme

Bibliographic information published by **Die Deutsche Bibliothek**.
Die Deutsche Bibliothek lists this publication in the 'Deutsche
Nationalbibliografie'; detailed bibliographic data is available on the Internet at
http://dnb.ddb.de/.

Cover concept and art by Christian J. Holoka
Cover design by Dutton & Sherman Design

The paper in this book meets the guidelines for permanence and durability
of the Committee on Production Guidelines for Book Longevity
of the Council of Library Resources.

© 2003, 2005, 2006, 2008 Peter Lang Publishing, Inc., New York
29 Broadway, 18th Floor, New York, NY 10006
www.peterlang.com

Printed in the United States of America

For Mary Ann

*Il est un amour personnel et humain qui est pur
et qui enferme un pressentiment
et un reflet de l'amour divin.*

❧

*There is a personal and human love that is pure
and that bears within it a presentiment
and a reflection of divine love.*

—Simone Weil

Contents

❧☙

Preface

My intention in this work is to provide a proper edition of Simone Weil's "L'*Iliade* ou le poème de la force." Though the essay has appeared in English translation in pamphlet form and in anthologies of her work, this is the first bilingual edition and the first based on the definitive 1989 *Œuvres complètes* text. It is also the only English version to give citations for passages quoted from the *Iliad*. (An Appendix provides the original Greek text of all the lines that Weil translates.) The Introduction briefly locates the piece within the corpus of Weil's writings and in the evolution of her philosophical and political thought. It also offers a review of critical assessments of the essay and examines its interpretive premises. Though it may seem otiose to attach a commentary to a composition written in Weil's most concise and perspicuous style, I have thought that a classicist might add to the significance of her interpretations by comparing them with the critiques of leading Homeric scholars. In addition, I have sought to highlight the "true to life" quality of many of Weil's reflections on Homeric warfare by juxtaposing them with accounts by or about modern soldiers. I hope that I have not gilded the lily.

Portions of the Introduction appeared in a different form in *Masterplots II: Nonfiction Series*, ed. Frank N. Magill (Pasadena, CA: Salem Press, 1989), pp. 684–88 and "Homer and Simone Weil: The *Iliad sub specie violentiae*" in *Epea pteroenta, Beiträge zur Homerforschung: Festschrift für Wolfgang Kullmann zum 75. Geburtstag*, ed. M. Reichel and A. Rengakos (Stuttgart: F. Steiner Verlag, 2002), pp. 63–75. For permission to print the definitive French text and a fresh translation, I am grateful to Éditions Gallimard, Paris.

To Eastern Michigan University I am indebted for the grant of a sabbatical leave to work on this book. I am also beholden to Eastern's

Graduate School, and especially to Dean Robert Holkeboer, for a Research Support Fund award at a critical juncture.

A number of friends and colleagues kindly shared their expertise and encouragement along the way, especially the patient current and former members of my department's French section: Brigitte Muller, Benjamin Palmer, Geneviève Peden, and Thomas Vosteen. In this project as in many others, Donald Lateiner offered valuable support and advice. My wife, Jo Ann, has again been my most careful and most caring editor. Remaining flaws and infelicities are entirely my own.

A Note on Translation

In describing the style of expression and argument of Simone Weil's "L'*Iliade* ou le poème de la force," I am tempted to recall the adjectives that Matthew Arnold famously applied to Homer himself: rapid, plain, direct, and noble. Such attributes make translation of the French both easy and difficult. Weil's word choice is straightforward: she uses no esoteric or pedantic vocabulary. Her syntax is uncomplicated, featuring short, frequently staccato sentences; clauses and phrases are linked like beads on a string, often with conjunctions replaced by semicolons. Coordination is favored over subordination. The final impression is of a penetrating simplicity, not oversimplification. For example, Weil writes of the petrifactive influence of force on certain of its victims: "Il est vivant, il a une âme; il est pourtant une chose" / "He is living, he has a soul; he is nonetheless a thing" (para. 7). Her prose style suits perfectly the sincerity and the urgency of the essay's message. I can only wish that I have retained some reflection of these traits in my translation.

Lines quoted from the *Iliad* are translated from Weil's French, not from the original Greek. I have only occasionally discussed semantic points about her translations in my commentary, in general preferring to let her versions stand as integral to the overall effect of the argumentation.

Citations of Homer's *Iliad* are by book and line numbers alone. For other primary sources relevant titles are indicated. Unattributed translations are my own, except for quotations of the Holy Bible, which are from the Revised English Bible.

Ypsilanti, Michigan   J.P.H.
1 January 2003

PART I

Introduction

The *Iliad*, composed ca. 725 B.C., stands at the very beginning of the western literary tradition. Its influence has been enormous right from the outset: it is clearly evident in the lyric poetry of the seventh and sixth centuries and in the tragic dramas of the fifth century. One thinks of Aeschylus's *bon mot* about his plays being "scraps from Homer's banquet."[1] And, of course, every epic poem in classical antiquity, from Vergil's sublime *Aeneid*[2] to the third-rate *Posthomerica* of Quintus Smyrnaeus, was heavily indebted to Homeric precedent. This literary influence reasserted itself in the Renaissance and has extended to such diverse twentieth-century authors as James Joyce, Nikos Kazantzakis, Christa Wolf, and Derek Walcott.

In addition to this strictly literary heritage, the vast enterprise of Homeric scholarship may have originated with an official Athenian recension of the *Iliad* and the *Odyssey* already in the later sixth century; it was certainly a professional fixation of the Alexandrian scholars of the Hellenistic period. In modern times, Friedrich August Wolf's *Prolegomena ad Homerum* (Halle 1795) was an opening shot in the often-bitter scholarly wars over the authorship, pre-history, and composition of Homer's works that have preoccupied academic research right up to the present day.[3]

Because the Homeric epics have been part of the furnishings of so many educated minds through the ages, the study of readers' responses to the poems is a fascinating exercise in intellectual history.[4] Some have seen the world presented by the Greek poet as primitive, barbaric, and quite alien from our own. Nietzsche, writing of the Greeks' "tigerish lust to annihilate," asked: "Why did the whole Greek world exult over the combat scenes of the *Iliad*? I fear that we do not understand them in a sufficiently 'Greek' manner; indeed, that

we should shudder if we were ever to understand them 'in Greek.'"[5]
Gilbert Murray thought that even those barbarities on display in the
epic had been toned down and reduced by expurgation.[6]

As is the case with most masterpieces of literature, however, many
readers have found in Homer a spirit contemporary with themselves.
"The foreignness between Homer and ourselves, apparent chiefly in
external forms, shrinks away in the face of the obvious constants
taken together.... Were Homer really foreign to us, then our present
world could hardly be recognized in him so consistently ...."[7]

An essay by a young woman writing in France during the Second
World War and reflecting on the nature of violence in human history
provides a remarkably vivid testament to this "nearness" of Homer.

Taken as a whole, Simone Weil's varied writings—which run to six-
teen volumes in the complete works series—are, like Walt Whitman's
poetry or Proust's grand novel, a chronicle of a long spiritual quest
undertaken by a peculiarly zealous personality. Although only thirty
years old when she wrote "The *Iliad* or the Poem of Force," Weil had
already addressed a wide range of fundamental philosophical issues
both academically and in the conduct of a personal life of often ago-
nizing inner conflict. The ardor she brought to her intellectual pur-
suits and to particular social and political causes that engaged her
energies have made her an attractive subject for biographers, as the
spate of works on her life and career in the last thirty years attests.[8]

Simone Weil (b. 1909) had a brilliant academic career: she placed
first in the nationwide entrance examination in General Philosophy
and Logic for the prestigious École Normale Supérieure in Paris. After graduation in 1931, she taught in a series of provincial lycées. At
the same time her absorption in the social, political, and economic realities of the world around her drew her for a time to Marxism,[9] with
which she became disenchanted, however, both because she despised
Stalinist totalitarianism and because Marxism finally seemed inadequate to explain or improve conditions either in Russia or in France.

> At a time when many intellectuals (including Camus) were joining the
> communist party in response to the crisis of capitalism and the rise of fas-
> cism, Simone Weil perceptively observed that Marxism and the Russian
> state provided an empty hope for the emancipation of the proletariat and
> that capitalism, fascism, and socialism were becoming in practice more

alike, as production in these forms of society came under the domination of a technocratic elite. She believed that many people had failed to see that Russia was not a workers' state in the sense that workers possessed democratic institutions, nor could it be in a "transitional" phase (as many had argued) when the workers were oppressed by a "bureaucratic caste." This failure, she argued, was due to the tendency to distinguish only between the two kinds of state, the capitalist and the workers', while the Russian regime was neither the one nor the other, but a new and oppressive form.[10]

Marxist or not, Weil continued to sympathize with the plight of the working poor. She participated in union activities on their behalf and even worked for short periods in factories and at a vineyard. In 1936, like many other idealistic intellectuals, she joined Republican forces in the Spanish Civil War, using a journalist's credentials, but "determined to do something more than just report the war."[11] Her service lasted less than two months, when she badly burned her leg in a cooking accident.

In 1938, a profound mystical experience[12] moved Weil toward a quest for spiritual truth. From childhood, a tough ascetic strain in her character compelled her to share—either actually or, more often, vicariously through self-denial—the privations of others, from impoverished factory workers to soldiers caught in the vise of war, to the subjugated populations of occupied lands. Over the years, this pathological self-discipline strained her health; she died of heart failure caused by pulmonary tuberculosis and self-starvation[13] on 24 August 1943, while working for the Free French during exile in London.

Through all these experiences, Weil recorded her thoughts in notebooks, journals, and a succession of published essays on social, political, philosophical, and theological matters: war and its causes, the claims and failings of various "-isms" (nationalism, militarism, capitalism, communism, fascism, totalitarianism), and the nature and ultimate source of spiritual enlightenment.

Most important as regards "The *Iliad* or the Poem of Force," Weil was also fascinated by the role of power in shaping human destiny. This was, understandably, especially prominent in her mind in the context of the Second World War,[14] and some have justifiably seen the essay as first and foremost "a document of its time: an extraordinary response to the war with Hitler and the fall of France, written by a Frenchwoman primarily for her compatriots in both occupied and unoccupied France ...."[15]

෯ ෯ ෯

Simone Weil's essay on Homer is not merely a foray into literary criticism. Merging several lines of inquiry—theological, philosophical, and political—with the literary, it attests to an abiding love for the Greek classics[16] and an unshakeable confidence in their enduring truths. More general reflections outline the wider implications of power in the social and political life of all times and places. As its overarching theme, the essay highlights the sinister psychological changes wrought by force upon both its victims and its momentary possessors.

"The true hero, the true subject matter, the center of the *Iliad* is force" (para. 1). The first sentence of "The *Iliad* or the Poem of Force" proclaims Weil's principal thesis with a typical directness. The essay advances this thesis by terse commentaries on particular Homeric passages, usually without any filling in of narrative context or even identification of characters being described. The piece is very lean in that sense. But the first paragraph also puts forth a second, less explicit contention as a subtext or corollary of the main argument. According to Weil, some readers have thought Homer's poem a historical document of a more primitive and more brutal stage of civilization, but "those wise enough to discern the force at the center of all human history, today as in the past, find in the *Iliad* the most beautiful and flawless of mirrors" (para. 1)—reflecting the social and political conditions of our own times as well. Force converts people literally into things, that is, corpses: "Someone was there and, the next moment, no one" (para. 2). Homer's masterpiece graphically depicts carnage, hundreds of individual deaths picked out in unflinching, grisly detail. While valiant Hector's mutilated body lies on the battlefield, his wife Andromache orders a hot bath for the husband who will never return: "he was far from warm baths, that hapless man," Weil observes, adding "nearly all human life has always taken place far from warm baths" (para. 6).

There is, however, a more subtly operative force: "that which does not kill, or rather does not kill just yet" (para. 7). Under this heading, Weil discusses the peculiar ontological status of the defeated man who supplicates his conqueror. Paralyzed by the imminence of deadly force, he impersonates in advance the nothingness that is his fate. Witnesses view the suppliant as they would a dead man, at first with a shudder, then with indifference. He has effectively ceased to exist even before the fatal sword stroke.

Besides suppliants, there are other, even more unfortunate inhabitants of the empire of force—the enslaved, who suffer a protracted death-in-life. Weil poignantly characterizes the plight of women and children taken in war: Chryseis, Briseis, and, as foreseen by Hector, Andromache and Astyanax. Each, forcibly deprived of expression and feeling, is consigned to "a life that death has frozen long before putting an end to it" (para. 14).

Weil's most sweeping claim about the world view of the *Iliad* is that Homer's "Poem of Force" demonstrates the pathetic debasement of all humans. The common soldier, like Thersites, is, in theory, a free agent but must endure the indignity of subordination and of abuse should he balk at orders. At the high end of the social scale, magnificent and invincible Achilles suffers humiliation at the hands of his superior, Agamemnon, who, in his turn, must shortly humble himself.

The relevance of this situation to later ages and to ourselves is clear to Weil: the persistence of warfare and other forms of violence throughout history has meant that, though force may victimize some later rather than sooner, some less patently than others, all without exception are drawn into its net. Force, like death, is the great leveler.[17] She insists that those who "possess" force do so only illusorily and always fleetingly. Warriors in the *Iliad* may enjoy short-lived triumphs, but they will eventually taste defeat. Achilles' death follows Hector's as surely as Hector's does that of Patroclus. The lesson is that "Ares is just and kills those who kill" (para. 33). But this lesson is lost on those so shortsighted and naïve as to believe they may control force while evading its fatal effects. "Those to whom fate has loaned force perish through their over-reliance on it" (para. 34). Weil stresses the pervasive Greek theme of Nemesis—violation of measure brings automatic retribution.

The informing political proposition of "The *Iliad* or the Poem of Force" is that the essential immoderation of force infects everyone it touches. Only a superhuman virtue could resist its allure. So it is that soldiers march to war with mindless enthusiasm. Victory in battle is itself an excess: "it is not usually political considerations that counsel excess. The temptation to excess is virtually irresistible" (para. 48). The countervailing voice of sweet reason, so rarely raised in the *Iliad*, falls always on deaf ears. The initial intoxication with force may endure for a time, but eventually and ineluctably the brutalities of defeat and death deform the souls of warriors. Men in war are caught in a horrific self-perpetuating cycle, so preoccupied with doing themselves violence as to perceive no escape. "The soul undergoes duress every day. Each morning it amputates itself of all aspiration, for thought cannot travel in time without encountering death" (para. 53). Because the inertia of force seems insuperable, the warrior sees only death in his future.

Weil discovers confirmation for this view of force in the *Iliad*'s many similes: again and again, Homer compares Greeks and Trojans to animals, to elements (sand, fire, flood, wind), to plants, in short "whatever is affected by the violence of outside forces" (para. 61). Force makes over human beings into objects, either corpses or breathing but soulless instruments. The same petrifactive quality is everywhere at work. She admits that "fleeting and sublime moments when men possess a soul" (para. 63) relieve the scenes of undiluted horror in the epic. At these times, we see a respect for the bonds of hospitality, the devotion of familial love, and even the possibility of friendship between mortal enemies. But such evanescent moments of grace only heighten our regret at the eclipse of human kindness in the world that force constructs.

Weil amplifies the tone of bitterness that suffuses the *Iliad*—a bitterness arising from the poet's tender sympathy for the fate of those trapped in the hellish conditions of war and the greatest of human calamities, the fall of a city. This sympathy bathes Greeks and Trojans alike in a light of love and justice.[18] No human eludes suffering; no suffering is contemptible. According to Weil, the Greeks alone developed such a view of the world and fashioned from it "the only true epic that the West possesses" (para. 81). Many, like Northrop Frye, have reached similar conclusions:

> It is hardly possible to overestimate the importance for Western literature of the *Iliad*'s demonstration that the fall of an enemy, no less than of a friend or leader, is tragic and not comic. With the *Iliad*, once for all, an objective and disinterested element enters into the poet's vision of human life. Without this element, poetry is merely instrumental to various social aims, to propaganda, to amusement, to devotion, to instruction; with it, it acquires the authority that since the *Iliad* it has never lost, an authority based, like the authority of science, on the vision of nature as an impersonal order.[19]

In a provocative assay of literature, Weil finds a vision akin to that of the *Iliad* in the plays of Aeschylus and Sophocles, and in the Gospels, which she considers "the final splendid expression of the Greek genius" (para. 82), but not in the *Odyssey*, the Old Testament, the *Aeneid*, or the *chansons de geste*. "The *Iliad* or the Poem of Force" ends with a sobering meditation on the failure of European literature to regain the Greek freedom from self-deception and to renew the epic genius. The lessons of Homer's epic—not to idolize force, not to despise the enemy, not to disdain the unfortunate, not to presume exemption from fate—remain for the peoples of Europe to learn.

Only in the ten or fifteen years after World War II did Simone Weil's thought become widely accessible through publication of her books, journals, notebooks, and articles. The essay on the *Iliad* was among the first of her works to appear in English.[20] Most readers see this study of Homer as an excursion into literary criticism by a thinker whose chief contributions and interests lay elsewhere. However, far from being merely a fascinating venture into a tangential area of inquiry, it shifted and sharpened the focus of her political and moral philosophy.[21]

> This meditation about war also offers insights for Weil into the workings of capitalist production. It helped her to develop a moral understanding of the damage done to the oppressed and afflicted that would otherwise be legitimized or at the very least rendered invisible.[22]

"The *Iliad* or the Poem of Force" has attracted its largest readership among students of literature and specifically of Homer, most of whom know little of Weil's other writings. For anyone who loves the Greek epic, the essay holds a special appeal. In the first place, its severe perspicuity and depth of feeling make it a convincing critique. Secondly, Weil's interpretation of the poem often comes as a revelation, since many readers have found (or have been taught to find) a delight in heroic warfare in the *Iliad*. It is often assumed that the poet's original audience must have relished the many scenes of combat between mighty warriors and that the epic should be read in this spirit. Weil undermines that conventional interpretation of the poem. Even if one does not accept completely the vision she attributes to Homer, the brilliance of her argument compels us to evaluate more

carefully the meaning of his poem. The handful of professional classical scholars who have noticed Weil's essay have generally admired
it,[23] though, like all her work, it is certainly free of the trappings of
specialized scholarship.

> Weil's reading is subjective. The essay disregards ... the historical condi-
> tions that surround the literary work. It cannot be viewed in the context of
> Homeric scholarship ..., since it does not deal either with textual problems
> or with the oral epic tradition. Nor does it represent any of the main cur-
> rents of twentieth-century literary criticism .... But the essay has made an
> impact, independently, by offering a communication with the original text
> that is immediate, philosophical and non-historical. Herein lies its interest.[24]

What are the theoretical bases of Weil's iconoclastic and often doc-
trinaire approach to the epic?   First and foremost, her critical
orientation is avowedly ethical: "Writers do not have to be professors
of morals, but they do have to express the human condition. And
nothing concerns human life so essentially, for every man at every
moment, as good and evil."[25] Authors must be appraised on the basis
of the moral grounds from which they write.[26] This goes against the
grain of much twentieth-century literary criticism: formalists, New
Critics, and structuralists stress the aesthetic or structural analysis of
the work and emulate the dispassion of scientific analysis by claiming
to eschew explicit moral judgments of a work's effect or an author's
motives; Marxists, proponents of deconstruction, and gender dis-
course critics stress the relations among author, text, and reader/critic
within shifting matrices of political and socioeconomic power.

Weil does forthrightly what most critics have always done tacitly
(despite their disavowals)—pass moral judgment on literary works.
Her candid stress on moral value is appealing and refreshing.

> After the current fad of French structuralism ... it would be a relief to find
> serious and thoughtful critics asking old-fashioned questions again, like "Is
> this true?" and "Does this help us do right in the world?" rather than "How
> intricately and cleverly is this put together?" I admire her attempt to bring
> "nonliterary" values to bear on the *Iliad*, even if they overwhelm it at
> times.[27]

Although ethical criticism, more than purely formalist or aesthetic
criticism, runs the risk of applying anachronistic or chauvinistic value
systems to a given work of art and has thus often fallen into disre-

pute, it has never really been eradicated from literary analysis. As Wayne Booth has put it,

> even those critics who work hard to purge themselves of all but the most abstract formal interests turn out to have an ethical program in mind—a belief that a given way of reading, or a given kind of genuine literature, is what will do us most good.[28]

Such criticism is commonplace and in any case inevitable, whether or not it is always appropriate.[29]

Weil trusted her own assessment of the "realities" of twentieth-century life, in particular, the oppression and privation ensuing from the idolatry of power. Our failure to appreciate the degrading dominance of power-corrupted social and governmental institutions imposed—in Weil's opinion—a pressing agenda on the literary artist. A literature that was "true" would expose the misguided allegiance of humankind to the corrosive ethos of force. This is why she felt that the *Iliad* was superior to the Hebrew scriptures,[30] in which a patriarchal deity condoned and abetted massacres.

> What filled her with indignation was the fact that the order for the extermination is presented in the Bible [1 Samuel 15:3] as God's order and that neither the person who wrote this story nor the majority of those who read it, including Christians, had found it repugnant to admit that God could give such an order.[31]

The author of the *Iliad*, Weil argues, neither lionizes victors nor denigrates losers; Homer well knows that force is the only winner, and all humans alike are its hostages. Even the gods, who appear to enjoy the questionable luxury of dispensing the short-lived "successes" of individuals and armies, are constrained by fate.[32] "One may not debase God to the point of making Him a partisan in war. The same applies to the Old Testament. There God is a partisan. In the *Iliad*, the gods are partisans, but Zeus takes up his golden scales."[33]

Similarly, Weil had a very low regard for the literature of ancient Rome,[34] produced, in her view, by an imperialistic people, and overtly committed to a mythology of empire.[35] The main theme of her "Reflections on the Origins of Hitlerism"[36] is the close resemblance between the ancient Roman and modern fascist states: "The analogy between the systems of Hitler and of ancient Rome is so striking that one might believe that Hitler alone, after two thousand years, has understood correctly how to copy the Romans."[37]

To the extent that Christianity evolved from Hebrew and Roman traditions, it, too, was infected with the idolatry of force. The early Christians were wrong to think grace could inoculate one against suffering: the martyrs did not have what Christ lacked. The soul may indeed survive but not unwounded by ultimate insight into human subjection to force. The Church, Weil noted, would even exert force to convert others, believing itself to be acting righteously; hence, another fatal blindness to the contagion of force.[38]

In Weil's comparative estimation of national literatures, only the Greeks (and they not invariably) recognized the threat force poses in human affairs and sympathized with, rather than despised, those whom it debased. This was a necessary attitude, since, for Weil, we are all without exception similarly vulnerable. With unhesitant frankness, she devalues the literary/moral merit of writers whose works fall short of the Greek standard:

> In Latin literature how seldom do we hear the humane accent which sounds so often in Homer, Aeschylus, Sophocles, and in Greek prose.... When they were not glorifying power the Latin poets, Lucretius and Juvenal always excepted, were chiefly concerned to sing of pleasure and love ... but the astonishing baseness of the elegists' conception of love is closely related, in all probability, to the worship of force, and it contributes to the overall impression of brutality.[39]

By contrast the *Iliad* furnishes a "mirror of reality" —socially, politically, morally.

Has Weil, by stressing the ancient poet's insistent disclosure of the dehumanizing consequences of force, made him our contemporary?[40] Has she read her own essentially Christian[41] values into the poem? And does not the epic, viewed with the disinterest of the historian, rather evince a celebration of force, by depicting the confrontations, the victories and defeats of heroic combatants struggling for honor on the battlefield?[42]

To answer such questions, one may examine the method of Weil's critical discussions. And in this regard, she is a largely persuasive commentator. She accumulates compelling evidence for her vision of the poem by appealing directly to the text.[43] For example, Homer in truth—in his "signature" similes—often likens human beings to forces of nature. That such equations—hundreds of them in the *Il-*

iad—have a powerful cumulative effect is indisputable. Similarly, there is the bludgeoning and repulsive impact on the reader of the poem in its entirety of the numerous, graphic scenes of mayhem and death on the battlefield.[44] A moral evaluation of the similes and battlefield descriptions invites the charge of subjectivity, but to the extent that we are entitled to formulate such interpretations of the text at all, Weil employs sound analytical procedures. She can, naturally, be convicted of specific errors of interpretation or understanding,[45] but we may not fault the methodology *per se* of her literary critical argumentation. She avoids vague impressionism by close reading.

A second approach is to place Weil's treatment of the poem's distinctive insight and artistry within her own political and philosophical points of view. In this sense, whether she is "right" in interpreting the poem's virtues as she does is beside the point.[46] As T.S. Eliot wrote,

> In trying to understand her, we must not be distracted—as is only too likely to happen on a first reading—by considering how far, and at what points, we agree or disagree. We must simply expose ourselves to the personality of a woman of genius, of a kind of genius akin to that of saints.... Our first experience of Simone Weil should not be expressible in terms of approval or dissent. I cannot conceive of anybody's agreeing with all of her views, or of not disagreeing violently with some of them. But agreement and rejection are secondary: what matters is to make contact with a great soul.[47]

The value of Weil's essay lies in her distinctive outlook on the human condition, quite apart from the accuracy of its representation of Homer's actual worldview (insofar as it may be recaptured). It transcends the goals of conventional historicist or positivistic literary analysis by affording both a novel interpretation[48] of an ancient masterpiece and an intrinsically valuable moral experience.[49]

Participating in Simone Weil's vision of Homer's "message," we benefit by her singular understanding of the relations of human beings and the effect of force on those relations. Her essay may not be "the purest mirror" of Homer's poem, but it certainly enlarges and improves our vision of the *Iliad*.

Notes

1   Athenaeus 8.347e.
2   To begin to appreciate the breadth and depth of Homer's influence on Vergil's epic, see the phenomenally detailed analysis in Knauer (1979).
3   See "A Historical Sketch of Homeric Scholarship," in Latacz (1996) 5–13, and Holoka (1991).
4   See Clarke (1981).
5   From "Homer's Contest," in Kaufmann (1954) 32–33.
6   Murray (1934) 128–29.
7   Latacz (1996) 21.
8   A thorough account of the particulars of Weil's life is that of her friend Simone Pétrement (1976); equally meticulous, less hagiographic, and stronger on her social and intellectual concerns is Nevin (1991). Fiori's "intellectual biography" (1989), though heavily reliant on Pétrement, adds additional information from interviews with relatives, friends, and associates of Weil still alive in the 1970s. Coles, in his speculative psychoanalytic discussion (1987), shows less familiarity with her philosophical thought. McLellan's study (1989) is especially insightful on the political dimensions of Weil's outlook. Dunaway (1984), Little (1988), Hourdin (1989), and Gray (2001) are valuable, briefer examinations of her life and writings.
9   Already at school, she had acquired from one of her professors (C. Bouglé) the sobriquet "Red Virgin"—see Pétrement (1976) 73–74, 77, 118.
10 Rosen (1979) 302.
11 Pétrement (1976) 269. Cf. Knox (1989) 290: "For those in Western Europe and America who viewed the steady advance of fascism with growing apprehension, and the spineless acquiescence of the British and French governments with contemptuous anger, the resistance of the Spanish people to the military rebellion was an inspiration and a challenge."
12 Weil (1951) 76–77: "In this sudden possession of me by Christ, neither my senses nor my imagination had any part; I only felt in the midst of my suffering the presence of love, like that which one can read in the smile on a beloved face.... I had never foreseen the possibility of ... a real contact, person to person, here below, between a human being and God." See Pétrement (1976) 340–42.
13 Pétrement (1976) 537: "The coroner issued a verdict of suicide.... The death certificate indicates that ... 'The deceased did kill and slay herself by refusing to eat whilst the balance of her mind was disturbed.' This is the formula ordinarily used in such cases, since suicide is prohibited by English law." But see Nevin (1991) 35: "Speculation as to whether she willed her death or wanted to die seems entirely useless, not to say morbid. Without doubt she faced the imminence of death with an acceptance that sometimes disconcerts healthy

onlookers. It does no violence to fact to suppose that that acceptance was her supreme gesture of *amor fati.*"

14 "L'*Iliade* ou le poème de la force" first appeared (under the anagrammatic pseudonym Emile Novis) December 1940/January 1941 in *Cahiers du Sud,* a journal published at Marseilles, where Weil had moved after the occupation of Paris. It was reprinted in *La Source grecque* (Weil [1953] 11–42) and has more recently been reissued in *Œuvres complètes* (Weil [1989] 227–253); for detailed discussion of its gestation and publication, see in the latter the Appendix on the "Genèse de l'article sur l'*Iliade*" (304–9).

15 Summers (1981) 87. Cf. Ferber (1981) 66: "She is not the only French writer of her generation to turn to the *Iliad* for insight into reality.... Someone who knows French and French literature ... ought to look into the possibility that the *Iliad* had an important part in the social and moral revaluation that took place during the Occupation and the postwar years"; Nevin (1991) x: ["The *Iliad* or the Poem of Force"] is not about Homer's Troy but about what war in the twentieth century should teach us. Its true context is not to be found at Ilium but at Compiègne in June 1940."

16 Weil studied Greek in her school days and taught Greek literature and language during her adult life. She carried in her memory large passages of Greek tragedy (Fiori [1989] 72), and was keenly aware of the nuances of Greek poetic diction, as may be seen throughout her notebooks and in her comments on translations of Homer by Victor Bérard and Paul Mazon in Weil (1965) 79, 92. She took great pains in translating into French the Homeric passages quoted in her essay on the *Iliad*: Pétrement (1976) 362, "The final result shows that this effort at precision was worth all the trouble. I believe that never before has a translation so completely captured the human tenderness and pity that pervades the *Iliad*."

17 Cf. McLane-Iles (1987) 91–92: "Beyond its punitive value, the displacement of power and force is the leveler of individuals. It is a form of geometrical symmetry which reduces us all to a common denominator."

18 Cf. Fraisse (1978) 196: "What she admires in Homer is that the poet is perfectly equitable toward both the conquerors and the vanquished; that is, he does not admire force"; and Clarke (1981) 293: "it is probably this equity, more than any other quality, that has ensured Homer's survival and success."

19 Frye (1957) 319.

20 Mary McCarthy's translation appeared in the November 1945 issue of *Politics* and has been frequently reprinted in pamphlet form—Weil (1956a). A translation by Elisabeth C. Geissbuhler appeared in Weil (1957) 24–55, rpt. in Panichas (1977) 153–83.

21 See K. Simonsuuri (1985) for a succinct discussion of how "Weil's writings on Greek literature and thought have ... a fundamental importance for the understanding of her work" (167).

22 Blum and Seidler (1989) 252; see, in general, their chapter on "Power" for penetrating and detailed analysis of the place of Weil's essay on Homer in the
structure of her *Weltanschauung*: "It was as if it was only with the careful reading of the *Iliad* ... and the Greek tragedies that Weil could touch an incom-
parably humane accent that they shared with the Gospels, if not with Christianity more generally" (216).

23 Colin W. Macleod (1982) 1, n. 1: "I know of no better brief account of the *Iliad*
than this"; so too, Griffin (1980) 193, n. 41, remarks that Weil's essay "seems to
me a profound and true account of the poem, and of other things besides."

24 Simonsuuri (1985) 167. See also O. Taplin (1980) 17 [(1991) 252, (1998) 112]:
"Simone Weil's essay ... was not written for scholars and is not argued in the
academic mode: it nonetheless conveys a fundamental understanding of the *Iliad*."

25 Weil (1968) 168–69.

26 Simonsuuri (1985) 166: "She represents a willingness to carry the crucial points
of her discussion far from the level of language and erudition to areas that are
more directly concerned with action and morality."

27 Ferber (1981) 81.

28 Booth (1988) 5.

29 See Booth (1988) 19: "We can no longer pretend that ethical criticism is passé. It
is practiced everywhere, often surreptitiously, often guiltily, and often badly,
partly because it is the most difficult of all critical modes, but partly because we
have so little serious talk about why it is important, what purposes it serves,
and how it might be done well." Simone Weil's essay on Homer is a striking example of such "serious talk."

30 See Weil (1977) 427: "The author of the *Iliad* depicts life as only a man who loves
God can see it. The author of Joshua as only a man who does not love God can
see it."

31 Pétrement (1976) 345–46. Weil's distaste for ancient Hebrew literature and for
Judaism and her relative silence on the plight of Jews in her own time have
prompted much comment and considerable controversy: Pétrement (1976) 554,
n. 6, Giniewski (1978), Isaiah Berlin (1980) 280: "there are symptoms of [Jewish
self-hatred] in the high-minded and deeply tormented essays of Simone Weil,"
Knopp (1984), Cruise (1986), Coles (1987) 42–62, Blum and Seidler (1989) 254–55,
Nevin (1991) 235–59, and Steiner (1993) 4: "In Weil's detestation of her own eth-
nic identity, in her strident denunciations of the cruelty and 'imperialism' of the
God of Abraham and Moses, in her very nearly hysterical repugnance in the
face of what she termed the excess of Judaism in the Catholicism she, finally, refused to join, the traits of classical Jewish self-loathing are carried to fever
pitch." For our purposes here, we need only be clear about the basis of Weil's
ethical criticism of literature.

32 Thus, Zeus briefly contemplates exempting his son Sarpedon from death at the hands of Patroclus until Hera forcefully reminds him of the demands of destiny: 16.431–57.

33 Weil (1956b) 55.

34 See Fraisse (1978) 193–95 for a good, brief discussion of anti-Roman bias among modern French writers: "[Weil] is heir ... to certain stereotypes of Greek beauty and purity, Roman perfidy, etc."

35 The prevailing attitude toward Golden Age Latin literature in Weil's day is exemplified in the chapter on "The Organization of Opinion" in Syme (1939): "Propaganda outweighed arms in the contests of the Triumviral period. Augustus' chief of cabinet, Maecenas, captured the most promising of the poets at an early stage and nursed them into the Principate.... As was fitting, the poets favoured by the government proceeded to celebrate in verse the ideals of renascent Rome—the land, the soldier, religion and morality, the heroic past and the glorious present.... The new Roman literature was designed to be civic rather than individual, more useful than ornamental" (460–61). Since the wars in Korea and Vietnam, many American classicists have perceived notes of ambivalence and skepticism in Roman poetry formerly thought essentially propagandistic. See, e.g., Parry's programmatic discussion (1963) and Putnam (1965) xiii: "The *Aeneid* ... must not be interpreted as a political tract in praise of Augustus or as a program for him to follow in the future but rather as a profound meditation on the necessities of historical development as seen through the eyes of a poet ... contemplating the exigencies demanded by rule and realizing the violations of personal integrity which necessarily follow in the wake of empire."

36 "Quelques réflexions sur les origines de l'Hitlérisme" (1939–1940), in Weil (1989) 168–219, translated in Weil (1962a).

37 Weil (1962a) 101 [(1989) 181]. Cf. Poole (1992) 1: "[Weil's] perilously racialist mythology incriminated the Roman and Hebraic strands in Western culture as the sources for the will to power that had driven the juggernaut of history. 'Hitlerism' was just Rome all over again: the rule of physical force, war as man's natural condition, the progressive annexing and erasing of all others and all otherness"; and Africa (1974) 187–88, n. 9: "The great German historian Theodor Mommsen saw [Julius] Caesar as a messianic hero who overthrew a cabal of corrupt reactionaries.... More recently, antifascist historians have damned the Roman dictator for the sins of the ersatz Caesars of the twentieth century." In Mussolini's Italy, the call to revive the glory of the ancient Roman Empire was a frequent refrain of fascist propaganda; see Mack Smith (1976).

38 Weil (1965) 129–30 [(1977) 83]: "I have never been able to understand how it is possible for a reasonable mind to regard the Jehovah of the Bible and the Father who is invoked in the Gospels as one and the same being. The influence of the Old Testament and of the Roman Empire, whose tradition was continued in the

Papacy, are to my mind the two essential sources of the corruption of Christianity."

39 Weil (1962a) 120.

40 Classical scholars have striven to abstain from intruding "anachronistic" values into interpretations of the thought and literature of classical antiquity. See, e.g., Lloyd-Jones (1961) 28: "If we carefully control every statement we make about an ancient theory or belief by reference to the evidence, if we are constantly on the watch against importing Christian or other modern preconceptions into antiquity ... we have a slender chance of getting at the truth"; but cf. Simonsuuri (1985) 169: "Gadamer talks, in *Wahrheit und Methode* (1960), about the need to avoid false topicality, the kind of relevance that is in fact typical of vulgarizing interpretations of literary works. But a new reading is a new text that expands the sphere of the work of art like a helix."

41 Weil (1977) 16: "all the *Iliad* is bathed in Christian light." The program implicit in Weil's explication of Homer's epic has, not surprisingly, drawn accusations of distortion and bias: Steiner (1969) 26 refers to Weil's essay as "a perverse reading of the *Iliad*"; Fiedler (1972) 11 speaks of "her splendid, though absurdly and deliberately partial, interpretation of the *Iliad*," and Clarke (1981) 293 of her "passionately one-sided reading of the *Iliad*."

42 See Steiner (1993) 4, who finds in Weil's essay "a bizarre interpretation ... a reading almost blind to the wild joy and ferocity of archaic warfare which makes the epic blaze ..."; also Edwards (1971).

43 See, e.g., Wilamowitz-Moellendorff (1969) 257: "We perform our task correctly only when we don't force our own mind into every ancient book that falls into our hands; but rather *read out of it what is already there*" [trans. W.M. Calder III; my emphasis].

44 See Fraisse (1978) 195–96: "A reading of the *Iliad* presents us a quite horrible succession of combats; in general, the *Iliad* is known in wonderful extracts—the encounter of Andromache and Hector, the entreaty of Priam to Achilles—that occupy an elevated moral and spiritual level. But when one reads the *Iliad* from beginning to end, the succession of battles and massacres is quite fatiguing." So too, Ferber (1981) 80–81: "While it may be interesting to learn how many ways a man may be done in by different weapons, such an interest is of a minute and morbid sort and no answer to the cumulative weight of death upon death. Perhaps Homer's original audience took delight in all the names and details, but it is hard to believe that they too did not feel the tedious burden of it all"; and Clarke (1981) 293: "there will be some who complain, with good reason, that the balances occasionally fail, that the *Iliad*'s battle scenes, for instance, run on too long ...."

45 See, e.g., Ferber (1981) 70–71, on a serious misreading of the Greek by Weil in her analysis of the interaction of Priam and Achilles in a crucial passage of Book 24; also Edwards (1987) 158: "Simone Weil's well-known account of the violence

in the *Iliad* ... presents only one side of the picture; most of the brutal statements she quotes are made by the characters, not by the poet, and she says nothing of the words of pathos and sympathy that follow so many of the killings"—but this overlooks that the similes she quotes as evidence are in the poet's voice.

46 See Simonsuuri (1985) 169, on Weil's essay as "a useful legitimate misreading of a kind that is vital for the tradition of literature;" and Nevin (1991) 133: "Weil chooses not to read Homer on what might be called Homeric terms."

47 T.S. Eliot, preface to Weil (1952b) vi. Cf. Poole (1992) 2: "Eliot presumably meant that the kind of exposure one incurs in reading Weil raises questions about one's deepest beliefs at a deeper level than more usual kinds of intellectual concurrence or divergence."

48 McLane-Iles (1987) 87–95 even brings Weil's criticism of Homer's epic fashionably up to date by seeing it in poststructuralist terms: "Weil uses the centrality of force to deconstruct the myth of heroism. The deconstruction of this myth, the leveling of all human character, serves to react against the reversal of Kantian priorities and to deconstruct the myth of power and false attributes" (90).

49 Cook (1953) 79: "She wrote no epics, yet neither was she guilty of any sort of fakery in her writing. True to her principles, she poured her spirit into every word and action, revealed the naked realities of the world with a most convincing combination of detachment and passion, and communicated to her readers (as they will testify) with a matchless simplicity of language."

PART II

L'*Iliade* ou le poème de la force

1. Le vrai héros, le vrai sujet, le centre de l'*Iliade*, c'est la force. La force qui est maniée par les hommes, la force qui soumet les hommes, la force devant quoi la chair des hommes se rétracte. L'âme humaine ne cesse pas d'y apparaître modifiée par ses rapports avec la force, entraînée, aveuglée par la force dont elle croit disposer, courbée sous la contrainte de la force qu'elle subit. Ceux qui avaient rêvé que la force, grâce au progrès, appartenait désormais au passé, ont pu voir dans ce poème un document; ceux qui savent discerner la force, aujourd'hui comme autrefois, au centre de toute histoire humaine, y trouvent le plus beau, le plus pur des miroirs.

2. La force, c'est ce qui fait de quiconque lui est soumis une chose. Quand elle s'exerce jusqu'au bout, elle fait de l'homme une chose au sens le plus littéral, car elle en fait un cadavre. Il y avait quelqu'un, et, un instant plus tard, il n'y a personne. C'est un tableau que l'*Iliade* ne se lasse pas de nous présenter:

> ... les chevaux
> Faisaient résonner les chars vides par les chemins de la guerre.
> En deuil de leurs conducteurs sans reproche. Eux sur terre
> Gisaient, aux vautours beaucoup plus chers qu' à leurs épouses.
>
> 11.159–62

3. Le héros est une chose traînée derrière un char dans la poussière:

> ... Tout autour, les cheveux
> Noirs étaient répandus, et la tête entière dans la poussière
> Gisait, naguère charmante; à présent Zeus à ses ennemis
> Avait permis de l'avilir sur sa terre natale.
>
> 22.401–4

4. L'amertume d'un tel tableau, nous la savourons pure, sans qu'-aucune fiction réconfortante vienne l'altérer, aucune immortalité consolatrice, aucune fade auréole de gloire ou de patrie.

> Son âme hors de ses membres s'envola, s'en alla chez Hadès,
> Pleurant sur son destin, quittant sa virilité et sa jeunesse.
>
> 22.362–63

5. Plus poignante encore, tant le contraste est douloureux, est l'évocation soudaine, aussitôt effacée, d'un autre monde, le monde lointain, précaire et touchant de la paix, de la famille, ce monde où chaque homme est pour ceux qui l'entourent ce qui compte le plus.

> Elle criait à ses servantes aux beaux cheveux par la demeure
> De mettre auprès du feu un grand trépied, afin qu'il y eût
> Pour Hector un bain chaud au retour du combat.
> La naïve! Elle ne savait pas que bien loin des bains chauds
> Le bras d'Achille l'avait soumis, à cause d'Athèna aux yeux verts.
>
> 22.442–46

6. Certes, il était loin des bains chauds, le malheureux. Il n'était pas le seul. Presque toute l'*Iliade* se passe loin des bains chauds. Presque toute la vie humaine s'est toujours passée loin des bains chauds.

7. La force qui tue est une forme sommaire, grossière de la force. Combien plus variée en ses procédés, combien plus surprenante en ses effets, est l'autre force, celle qui ne tue pas; c'est-à-dire celle qui ne tue pas encore. Elle va tuer sûrement, ou elle va tuer peut-être, ou bien elle est seulement suspendue sur l'être qu'à tout instant elle peut tuer; de toute façon, elle change l'homme en pierre. Du pouvoir de transformer un homme en chose en le faisant mourir procède un autre pouvoir, et bien autrement prodigieux, celui de faire une chose d'un homme qui reste vivant. Il est vivant, il a une âme; il est pourtant une chose. Être bien étrange qu'une chose qui a une âme; étrange état pour l'âme. Qui dira combien il lui faut à tout instant, pour s'y conformer, se tordre et se plier sur elle-même? Elle n'est pas faite pour habiter une chose; quand elle y est contrainte, il n'est plus rien en elle qui ne souffre violence.

8. Un homme désarmé et nu sur lequel se dirige une arme devient cadavre avant d'être touché. Un moment encore il combine, agit, espère:

> Il pensait, immobile. L'autre approche, tout saisi,
> Anxieux de toucher ses genoux. Il voulait dans son cœur

Échapper à la mort mauvaise, au destin noir ....
Et d'un bras il étreignait pour le supplier ses genoux,
De l'autre il maintenait la lance aiguë sans la lâcher ....

21.64–66, 71–72

9. Mais bientôt il a compris que l'arme ne se détournera pas, et, respirant encore, il n'est plus que matière, encore pensant ne peut plus rien penser:

Ainsi parla ce fils si brillant de Priam
En mots qui suppliaient. Il entendit une parole inflexible: ...
Il dit; à l'autre défaillent les genoux et le cœur;
Il lâche la lance et tombe assis, les mains tendues,
Les deux mains. Achille dégaine son glaive aigu,
Frappe à la clavicule, le long du cou; et tout entier
Plonge le glaive à deux tranchants. Lui, sur la face, à terre
Gît étendu, et le sang noir s'écoule en humectant la terre.

21.97–98, 114–19

10. Quand, hors de tout combat, un étranger faible et sans armes supplie un guerrier, il n'est pas de ce fait condamné à mort; mais un instant d'impatience de la part du guerrier suffirait à lui ôter la vie. C'est assez pour que sa chair perde la principale propriété de la chair vivante. Un morceau de chair vivante manifeste la vie avant tout par le sursaut; une patte de grenouille, sous le choc électrique, sursaute; l'aspect proche ou le contact d'une chose horrible ou terrifiante fait sursauter n'importe quel paquet de chair, de nerfs et de muscles. Seul, un pareil suppliant ne tressaille pas, ne frémit pas; il n'en a plus licence; ses lèvres vont toucher l'objet pour lui le plus chargé d'horreur:

On ne vit pas entrer le grand Priam. Il s'arrêta,
Étreignit les genoux d'Achille, baisa ses mains,
Terribles, tueuses d'hommes, qui lui avaient massacré tant de fils.

24.477–79

11. Le spectacle d'un homme réduit à ce degré de malheur glace à peu près comme glace l'aspect d'un cadavre:

Comme quand le dur malheur saisit quelqu'un, lorsque dans son pays
Il a tué, et qu'il arrive à la demeure d'autrui,
De quelque riche; un frisson saisit ceux qui le voient;
Ainsi Achille frissonna en voyant le divin Priam.
Les autres aussi frissonnèrent, se regardant les uns les autres.

24.480–84

12. Mais ce n'est qu'un moment, et bientôt la présence même du

malheureux est oubliée:

> Il dit. L'autre, songeant à son père, désira le pleurer;
> Le prenant par le bras, il poussa un peu le vieillard.
> Tous deux se souvenaient, l'un d'Hector tueur d'hommes,
> Et il fondait en larmes aux pieds d'Achille, contre la terre;
> Mais Achille, lui, pleurait son père, et par moments aussi
> Patrocle; leurs sanglots emplissaient la demeure.

24.507-12

13. Ce n'est pas par insensibilité qu'Achille a d'un geste poussé à terre le vieillard collé contre ses genoux; les paroles de Priam évoquant son vieux père l'ont ému jusqu'aux larmes. Tout simplement il se trouve être aussi libre dans ses attitudes, dans ses mouvements, que si au lieu d'un suppliant c'était un objet inerte qui touchait ses genoux. Les êtres humains autour de nous ont par leur seule présence un pouvoir, et qui n'appartient qu'à eux, d'arrêter, de réprimer, de modifier chacun des mouvements que notre corps esquisse; un passant ne détourne pas notre marche sur une route de la même manière qu'un écriteau, on ne se lève pas, on ne marche pas, on ne se rassied pas dans sa chambre quand on est seul de la même manière que lorsqu'on a un visiteur. Mais cette influence indéfinissable de la présence humaine n'est pas exercée par les hommes qu'un mouvement d'impatience peut priver de la vie avant même qu'une pensée ait eu le temps de les condamner à mort. Devant eux les autres se meuvent comme s'ils n'étaient pas là; et eux à leur tour, dans le danger où ils se trouvent d'être en un instant réduits à rien, ils imitent le néant. Poussés ils tombent, tombés demeurent à terre, aussi longtemps que le hasard ne fait pas passer dans l'esprit de quelqu'un la pensée de les relever. Mais qu'enfin relevés, honorés de paroles cordiales, ils ne s'avisent pas de prendre au sérieux cette résurrection, d'oser exprimer un désir; une voix irritée les ramènerait aussitôt au silence:

> Il dit, et le vieillard trembla et obéit.

24.571

14. Du moins les suppliants, une fois exaucés, redeviennent-ils des hommes comme les autres. Mais il est des êtres plus malheureux qui, sans mourir, sont devenus des choses pour toute leur vie. Il n'y a dans leurs journées aucun jeu, aucun vide, aucun champ libre pour rien qui vienne d'eux-mêmes. Ce ne sont pas des hommes vivant plus dure-

ment que d'autres, placés socialement plus bas que d'autres; c'est une autre espèce humaine, un compromis entre l'homme et le cadavre. Qu'un être humain soit une chose, il y a là, du point de vue logique, contradiction; mais quand l'impossible est devenu une réalité, la contradiction devient dans l'âme déchirement. Cette chose aspire à tous moments à être un homme, une femme, et à aucun moment n'y parvient. C'est une mort qui s'étire tout au long d'une vie; une vie que la mort a glacée longtemps avant de l'avoir supprimée.

15. La vierge, fille d'un prêtre, subira ce sort:

Je ne la rendrai pas. Auparavant la vieillesse l'aura prise,
Dans notre demeure, dans Argos, loin de son pays,
À courir devant le métier, à venir vers mon lit.

$$1.29\text{–}31$$

16. La jeune femme, la jeune mère, épouse du prince, le subira:

Et peut-être un jour dans Argos tu tisseras la toile pour une autre
Et tu porteras l'eau de la Messéis ou l'Hypérée,
Bien malgré toi, sous la pression d'une dure nécessité.

$$6.456\text{–}58$$

17. L'enfant héritier du sceptre royal le subira:

Elles sans doute s'en iront au fond des vaisseaux creux,
Moi parmi elles; toi, mon enfant, ou avec moi
Tu me suivras et tu feras d'avilissants travaux,
Peinant aux yeux d'un maître sans douceur ....

$$24.731\text{–}34$$

18. Un tel sort, aux yeux de la mère, est aussi redoutable pour son enfant que la mort même; l'époux souhaite avoir péri avant d'y voir sa femme réduite; le père appelle tous les fléaux du ciel sur l'armée qui y soumet sa fille. Mais chez ceux sur qui il s'abat, un destin si brutal efface les malédictions, les révoltes, les comparaisons, les méditations sur l'avenir et le passé, presque le souvenir. Il n'appartient pas à l'esclave d'être fidèle à sa cité et à ses morts.

19. C'est quand souffre ou meurt l'un de ceux qui lui ont fait tout perdre, qui ont ravagé sa ville, massacré les siens sous ses yeux, c'est alors que l'esclave pleure. Pourquoi non? Alors seulement les pleurs lui sont permis. Ils sont même imposés. Mais dans la servitude, les larmes ne sont-elles pas prêtes à couler dès qu'elles le peuvent impunément?

Elle dit en pleurant, et les femmes de gémir,

Prenant prétexte de Patrocle, chacune sur ses propres angoisses.

19.301–2

20. En aucune occasion l'esclave n'a licence de rien exprimer, sinon ce qui peut complaire au maître. C'est pourquoi si, dans une vie aussi morne, un sentiment peut poindre et l'animer un peu, ce ne peut être que l'amour du maître; tout autre chemin est barré au don d'aimer, de même que pour un cheval attelé les brancards, les rênes, le mors barrent tous les chemins sauf un seul. Et si par miracle apparaît l'espoir de redevenir un jour, par faveur, quelqu'un, à quel degré n'iront pas se porter la reconnaissance et l'amour pour des hommes envers qui un passé tout proche encore devrait inspirer de l'horreur:

> Mon époux, à qui m'avaient donnée mon père et ma mère respectée,
> Je l'ai vu devant ma cité transpercer par l'airain aigu.
> Mes trois frères, que m'avait enfantés une seule mère,
> Si chéris! ils ont trouvé le jour fatal.
> Mais tu ne m'as pas laissée, quand mon mari par le rapide Achille
> Fut tué, et détruite la cité du divin Mynès,
> Verser des larmes; tu m'as promis que le divin Achille
> Me prendrait pour femme légitime et m'emmènerait dans ses vaisseaux
> En Phthia, célébrer le mariage parmi les Myrmidons.
> Aussi sans répit je te pleure, toi qui as toujours été doux.

19.291–300

21. On ne peut perdre plus que ne perd l'esclave; il perd toute vie intérieure. Il n'en retrouve un peu que lorsqu'apparaît la possibilité de changer de destin. Tel est l'empire de la force: cet empire va aussi loin que celui de la nature. La nature aussi, lorsqu'entrent en jeu les besoins vitaux, efface toute vie intérieure et même la douleur d'une mère:

> Car même Niobé aux beaux cheveux a songé à manger,
> Elle à qui douze enfants dans sa maison périrent,
> Six filles et six fils à la fleur de leur âge.
> Eux, Apollon les tua avec son arc d'argent
> Dans sa colère contre Niobé; elles, Artémis qui aime les flèches.
> C'est qu'elle s'était égalée à Léto aux belles joues,
> Disant "elle a deux enfants; moi, j'en ai enfanté beaucoup."
> Et ces deux, quoiqu'ils ne fussent que deux, les ont fait tous mourir.
> Eux neuf jours furent gisants dans la mort; nul ne vint
> Les enterrer. Les gens étaient devenus des pierres par le vouloir de Zeus.
> Et eux le dixième jour furent ensevelis par les dieux du ciel.
> Mais elle a songé à manger, quand elle fut fatiguée des larmes.

24.602–13

22. On n'a jamais exprimé avec tant d'amertume la misère de l'homme, qui le rend même incapable de sentir sa misère.

23. La force maniée par autrui est impérieuse sur l'âme comme la faim extrême, dès qu'elle consiste en un pouvoir perpétuel de vie et de mort. Et c'est un empire aussi froid, aussi dur que s'il était exercé par la matière inerte. L'homme qui se trouve partout le plus faible est au cœur des cités aussi seul, plus seul que ne peut l'être l'homme perdu au milieu d'un désert.

> Deux tonneaux se trouvent placés au seuil de Zeus,
> Où sont les dons qu'il donne, mauvais dans l'un, bons dans l'autre ....
> À qui il fait des dons funestes, il l'expose aux outrages;
> L'affreux besoin le chasse au travers de la terre divine;
> Il erre et ne reçoit d'égards ni des hommes ni des dieux.

24.527–28, 531–33

24. Aussi impitoyablement la force écrase, aussi impitoyablement elle enivre quiconque la possède, ou croit la posséder. Personne ne la possède véritablement. Les hommes ne sont pas divisés, dans l'*Iliade*, en vaincus, en esclaves, en suppliants d'un côte, et en vainqueurs, en chefs, de l'autre; il ne s'y trouve pas un seul homme qui ne soit à quelque moment contraint de plier sous la force. Les soldats, bien que libres et armés, n'en subissent pas moins ordres et outrages:

> Tout homme du peuple qu'il voyait et prenait à crier,
> De son sceptre il le frappait et le réprimandait ainsi:
> "Misérable, tiens-toi tranquille, écoute parler les autres,
> Tes supérieurs. Tu n'as ni courage ni force,
> Tu comptes pour rien dans le combat, pour rien dans l'assemblée ...."

2.198–202

25. Thersite paie cher des paroles pourtant parfaitement raisonnables, et qui ressemblent à celles que prononce Achille.

> Il le frappa; lui se courba, ses larmes coulèrent pressées,
> Une tumeur sanglante sur son dos se forma
> Sous le sceptre d'or; il s'assit et eut peur.
> Dans la douleur et la stupeur il essuyait ses larmes.
> Les autres, malgré leur peine, y prirent plaisir et rirent.

2.266–70

26. Mais Achille même, ce héros fier, invaincu, nous est montré dès le début du poème pleurant d'humiliation et de douleur impuissante, après qu'on a enlevé sous ses yeux la femme dont il voulait faire son épouse, sans qu'il ait osé s'y opposer.

… Mais Achille
En pleurant s'assit loin des siens, à l'écart,
Au bord des vagues blanchissantes, le regard sur la mer vineuse.

1.348–50

27. Agamemnon a humilié Achille de propos délibéré, pour montrer qu'il est le maître:

… Comme cela, tu sauras
Que je peux plus que toi, et tout autre hésitera
À me traiter d'égal et à me tenir tête.

1.185–87

28. Mais quelques jours après le chef suprême pleure à son tour, est forcé de s'abaisser, de supplier, et il a la douleur de le faire en vain.

29. La honte de la peur non plus n'est pas épargnée à un seul des combattants. Les héros tremblent comme les autres. Il suffit d'un défi d'Hector pour consterner tous les Grecs sans aucune exception, sauf Achille et les siens qui sont absents:

Il dit, et tous se turent et gardèrent le silence;
Ils avaient honte de refuser, peur d'accepter.

7.92–93

30. Mais dès qu'Ajax s'avance, la peur change de côté:

Les Troyens, un frisson de terreur fit défaillir leurs membres;
Hector lui-même, son cœur bondit dans sa poitrine;
Mais il n'avait plus licence de trembler, ni de se réfugier ….

7.215–17

31. Deux jours plus tard, Ajax ressent à son tour la terreur:

Zeus le père, de là-haut, dans Ajax fait monter la peur.
Il s'arrête, saisi, derrière lui met le bouclier à sept peaux,
Tremble, regarde tout égaré la foule, comme une bête ….

11.544–46

32. À Achille lui-même il arrive une fois de trembler et de gémir de peur, devant un fleuve, il est vrai, non devant un homme. Lui excepté, absolument tous nous sont montrés à quelque moment vaincus. La valeur contribue moins à déterminer la victoire que le destin aveugle, représenté par la balance d'or de Zeus.

À ce moment Zeus le père déploya sa balance en or.
Il y plaça deux sorts de la mort qui fauche tout,

Un pour les Troyens dompteurs de chevaux, un pour les Grecs bardés d'airain.
Il la prit au milieu, ce fut le jour fatal des Grecs qui s'abaissa.

8.69–72

33. À force d'être aveugle, le destin établit une sorte de justice, aveugle elle aussi, qui punit les hommes armés de la peine du talion; l'*Iliade* l'a formulée longtemps avant l'Évangile, et presque dans les mêmes termes:

Arès est équitable, et il tue ceux qui tuent.

18.309

34. Si tous sont destinés en naissant à souffrir la violence, c'est là une vérité à laquelle l'empire des circonstances ferme les esprits des hommes. Le fort n'est jamais absolument fort, ni le faible absolument faible, mais l'un et l'autre l'ignorent. Ils ne se croient pas de la même espèce; ni le faible ne se regarde comme le semblable du fort, ni il n'est regardé comme tel. Celui qui possède la force marche dans un milieu non résistant, sans que rien, dans la matière humaine autour de lui, soit de nature à susciter entre l'élan et l'acte ce bref intervalle où se loge la pensée. Où la pensée n'a pas de place, la justice ni la prudence n'en ont. C'est pourquoi ces hommes armés agissent durement et follement. Leur arme s'enfonce dans un ennemi désarmé qui est à leurs genoux; ils triomphent d'un mourant en lui décrivant les outrages que son corps va subir; Achille égorge douze adolescents troyens sur le bûcher de Patrocle aussi naturellement que nous coupons des fleurs pour une tombe. En usant de leur pouvoir, ils ne se doutent jamais que les conséquences de leurs actes les feront plier à leur tour. Quand on peut d'un mot faire taire, trembler, obéir un vieillard, réfléchit-on que les malédictions d'un prêtre ont de l'importance aux yeux des devins? S'abstient-on d'enlever la femme aimée d'Achille, quand on sait qu'elle et lui ne pourront qu'obéir? Achille, quand il jouit de voir fuir les misérables Grecs, peut-il penser que cette fuite, qui durera et finira selon sa volonté, va faire perdre la vie à son ami et à lui-même? C'est ainsi que ceux à qui la force est prêtée par le sort périssent pour y trop compter.

35. Il ne se peut pas qu'ils ne périssent. Car ils ne considèrent pas leur propre force comme une quantité limitée, ni leurs rapports avec autrui comme un équilibre entre forces inégales. Les autres hommes n'imposant pas à leurs mouvements ce temps d'arrêt d'où seul procèdent nos égards envers nos semblables, ils en concluent que le

destin leur a donné toute licence, et aucune à leurs inférieurs. Dès lors ils vont au-delà de la force dont ils disposent. Ils vont inévitablement au-delà, ignorant qu'elle est limitée. Ils sont alors livrés sans recours au hasard, et les choses ne leur obéissent plus. Quelquefois le hasard les sert; d'autres fois il leur nuit; les voilà exposés nus au malheur, sans l'armure de puissance qui protégeait leur âme, sans plus rien désormais qui les sépare des larmes.

36. Ce châtiment d'une rigueur géométrique, qui punit automatiquement l'abus de la force, fut l'objet premier de la méditation chez les Grecs. Il constitue l'âme de l'épopée; sous le nom de Némésis, il est le ressort des tragédies d'Eschyle; les Pythagoriciens, Socrate, Platon, partirent de là pour penser l'homme et l'univers. La notion en est devenue familière partout où l'hellénisme a pénétré. C'est cette notion grecque peut-être qui subsiste, sous le nom de kharma, dans des pays d'Orient imprégnés de bouddhisme; mais l'Occident l'a perdue et n'a plus même dans aucune de ses langues de mot pour l'exprimer; les idées de limite, de mesure, d'équilibre, qui devraient déterminer la conduite de la vie, n'ont plus qu'un emploi servile dans la technique. Nous ne sommes géomètres que devant la matière; les Grecs furent d'abord géomètres dans l'apprentissage de la vertu.

37. La marche de la guerre, dans l'*Iliade*, ne consiste qu'en ce jeu de bascule. Le vainqueur du moment se sent invincible, quand même il aurait quelques heures plus tôt éprouvé la défaite; il oublie d'user de la victoire comme d'une chose qui passera. Au bout de la première journée de combat que raconte l'*Iliade*, les Grecs victorieux pourraient sans doute obtenir l'objet de leurs efforts, c'est-à-dire Hélène et ses richesses; du moins si l'on suppose, comme fait Homère, que l'armée grecque avait raison de croire Hélène dans Troie. Les prêtres égyptiens, qui devaient le savoir, affirmèrent plus tard à Hérodote qu'elle se trouvait en Égypte. De toutes manières, ce soir-là, les Grecs n'en veulent plus:

"Qu'on n'accepte à présent ni les biens de Pâris,
Ni Hélène; chacun voit, même le plus ignorant,
Que Troie est à présent sur le bord de la perte."
Il dit; tous acclamèrent parmi les Achéens.

7.400–403

38. Ce qu'ils veulent, ce n'est rien de moins que tout. Toutes les richesses de Troie comme butin, tous les palais, les temples et les mai-

sons comme cendres, toutes les femmes et tous les enfants comme esclaves, tous les hommes comme cadavres. Ils oublient un détail; c'est
que tout n'est pas en leur pouvoir; car ils ne sont pas dans Troie.
Peut-être ils y seront demain; peut-être ils n'y seront pas.

39. Hector, le même jour, se laisse aller au même oubli:

> Car je sais bien ceci dans mes entrailles et dans mon cœur;
> Un jour viendra où périra la sainte Ilion,
> Et Priam, et la nation de Priam à la bonne lance.
> Mais je pense moins à la douleur qui se prépare pour les Troyens,
> Et à Hécube elle-même, et à Priam le roi,
> Et à mes frères qui, si nombreux et si braves,
> Tomberont dans la poussière sous les coups des ennemis,
> Qu'à toi, quand l'un des Grecs à la cuirasse d'airain
> Te traînera toute en larmes, t'ôtant la liberté….
> Mais moi, que je sois mort et que la terre m'ait recouvert
> Avant que je t'entende crier, que je te voie traînée.

6.447–55, 464–65

40. Que n'offrirait-il pas à ce moment pour écarter des horreurs
qu'il croit inévitables? Mais il ne peut rien offrir qu'en vain. Le surlendemain les Grecs fuient misérablement, et Agamemnon même
voudrait reprendre la mer. Hector qui, en cédant peu de choses, ob-
tiendrait alors facilement le départ de l'ennemi, ne veut même plus
lui permettre de partir les mains vides:

> Brûlons partout des feux et que l'éclat en monte au ciel
> De peur que dans la nuit les Grecs aux longs cheveux
> Pour s'enfuir ne s'élancent au large dos des mers …
> Que plus d'un ait un trait même chez lui à digérer,
> … afin que tout le monde redoute
> De porter aux Troyens dompteurs de chevaux la guerre qui fait pleurer.

8.509–11, 513, 515–16

41. Son désir est réalisé; les Grecs restent; et le lendemain, à midi,
ils font de lui et des siens un objet pitoyable:

> Eux, à travers la plaine ils fuyaient comme des vaches
> Qu'un lion chasse devant lui, venu au milieu de la nuit ….
> Ainsi les poursuivait le puissant Atride Agamemnon,
> Tuant sans arrêt le dernier; eux, ils fuyaient.

11.172–73, 177–78

42. Dans le cours de l'après-midi, Hector reprend le dessus, recule
encore, puis met les Grecs en déroute, puis est repoussé par Patrocle

et ses troupes fraîches. Patrocle, poursuivant son avantage au-delà de ses forces, finit par se trouver exposé, sans armure et blessé, à l'épée d'Hector, et, le soir, Hector victorieux accueille par de dures réprimandes l'avis prudent de Polydamas:

> "À présent que j'ai reçu du fils de Cronos rusé
> La gloire auprès des vaisseaux, acculant à la mer les Grecs,
> imbécile! ne propose pas de tels conseils devant le peuple.
> Aucun Troyen ne t'écoutera; moi, je ne le permettrais pas."...
> Ainsi parla Hector, et les Troyens de l'acclamer ....

18.293–96, 310

43. Le lendemain Hector est perdu. Achille l'a fait reculer à travers toute la plaine et va le tuer. Il a toujours été le plus fort des deux au combat; combien davantage après plusieurs semaines de repos, emporté par la vengeance et la victoire, contre un ennemi épuisé! Voilà Hector seul devant les murs de Troie, complètement seul, à attendre la mort et à essayer de résoudre son âme à lui faire face.

> Hélas! si je passais derrière la porte et le rempart,
> Polydamas d'abord me donnerait de la honte ...
> Maintenant que j'ai perdu les miens par ma folie,
> Je crains les Troyens et les Troyennes aux voiles traînants
> Et que je n'entende dire par de moins braves que moi:
> "Hector, trop confiant dans sa force, a perdu le pays."...
> Si pourtant je posais mon bouclier bombé,
> Mon bon casque, et, appuyant ma lance au rempart,
> Si j'allais vers l'illustre Achille, à sa rencontre?...
> Mais pourquoi donc mon cœur me donne-t-il ces conseils?
> Je ne l'approcherais pas; il n'aurait pas pitié,
> Pas d'égard; il me tuerait, si j'étais ainsi nu,
> Comme une femme ....

22.99–100, 104–7, 111–13, 122–25

44. Hector n'échappe à aucune des douleurs et des hontes qui sont la part des malheureux. Seul, dépouillé de tout prestige de force, le courage qui l'a maintenu hors des murs ne le préserve pas de la fuite:

> Hector, en le voyant, fut pris de tremblement. Il ne put se résoudre
> À demeurer ....
> ... Ce n'est pas pour une brebis ou pour une peau de bœuf
> Qu'ils s'efforcent, récompenses ordinaires de la course;
> C'est pour une vie qu'ils courent, celle d'Hector dompteur de chevaux.

22.136–37, 159–61

45. Blessé à mort, il augmente le triomphe du vainqueur par des

supplications vaines:

Je t'implore par ta vie, par tes genoux, par tes parents ....

22.338

46. Mais les auditeurs de l'*Iliade* savaient que la mort d'Hector devait donner une courte joie à Achille, et la mort d'Achille une courte joie aux Troyens, et l'anéantissement de Troie une courte joie aux Achéens.

47. Ainsi la violence écrase ceux qu'elle touche. Elle finit par apparaître extérieure à celui qui la manie comme à celui qui la souffre; alors naît l'idée d'un destin sous lequel les bourreaux et les victimes sont pareillement innocents, les vainqueurs et les vaincus frères dans la même misère. Le vaincu est une cause de malheur pour le vainqueur comme le vainqueur pour le vaincu.

Un seul fils lui est né, pour une vie courte; et même,
Il vieillit sans mes soins, puisque bien loin de la patrie,
Je reste devant Troie à faire du mal à toi et à tes fils.

24.540–42

48. Un usage modéré de la force, qui seul permettrait d'échapper à l'engrenage, demanderait une vertu plus qu'humaine, aussi rare qu'une constante dignité dans la faiblesse. D'ailleurs la modération non plus n'est pas toujours sans péril; car le prestige, qui constitue la force plus qu'aux trois quarts, est fait avant tout de la superbe indifférence du fort pour les faibles, indifférence si contagieuse qu'elle se communique à ceux qui en sont l'objet. Mais ce n'est pas d'ordinaire une pensée politique qui conseille l'excès. C'est la tentation de l'excès qui est presque irrésistible. Des paroles raisonnables sont parfois prononcées dans l'*Iliade*; celles de Thersite le sont au plus haut degré. Celles d'Achille irrité le sont aussi:

Rien ne me vaut la vie, même tous les biens qu'on dit
Que contient Ilion, la cité si prospère ....
Car on peut conquérir les bœufs, les gras moutons ....
Une vie humaine, une fois partie, ne se reconquiert plus.

9.401–2, 406, 408

49. Mais les paroles raisonnables tombent dans le vide. Si un inférieur en prononce, il est puni et se tait; si c'est un chef, il n'y conforme pas ses actes. Et il se trouve toujours au besoin un dieu pour conseiller la déraison. À la fin l'idée même qu'on puisse vouloir échapper à l'occupation donnée par le sort en partage, celle de tuer et

de mourir, disparaît de l'esprit:

> ... nous à qui Zeus
> Dès la jeunesse a assigné, jusqu'à la vieillesse, de peiner
> Dans de douloureuses guerres, jusqu'à ce que nous périssions
>   jusqu'au dernier.

14.85–87

50. Ces combattants déjà, comme si longtemps plus tard ceux de Craonne, se sentaient "tous condamnés."

51. Ils sont tombés dans cette situation par le piège le plus simple. Au départ, leur cœur est léger comme toujours quand on a pour soi une force et contre soi le vide. Leurs armes sont dans leurs mains; l'ennemi est absent. Excepté quand on a l'âme abattue par la réputation de l'ennemi, on est toujours beaucoup plus fort qu'un absent. Un absent n'impose pas le joug de la nécessité. Nulle nécessité n'apparaît encore à l'esprit de ceux qui s'en vont ainsi, et c'est pourquoi ils s'en vont comme pour un jeu, comme pour un congé hors de la contrainte quotidienne.

> Où sont parties nos vantardises, quand nous nous affirmions si braves,
> Celles qu'à Lemnos vaniteusement vous déclamiez,
> En vous gorgeant des chairs des bœufs aux cornes droites,
> En buvant dans les coupes qui débordaient de vin?
> Qu'à cent ou à deux cents de ces Troyens chacun
> Tiendrait tête au combat; et voilà qu'un seul est trop pour nous!

8.229–34

52. Même une fois éprouvée, la guerre ne cesse pas aussitôt de sembler un jeu. La nécessité propre à la guerre est terrible, toute autre que celle liée aux travaux de la paix; l'âme ne s'y soumet que lorsqu'elle ne peut plus y échapper; et tant qu'elle y échappe elle passe des jours vides de nécessité, des jours de jeu, de rêve, arbitraires et irréels. Le danger est alors une abstraction, les vies qu'on détruit sont comme des jouets brisés par un enfant et aussi indifférentes; l'héroïsme est une pose de théâtre et souillé de vantardise. Si de plus, pour un moment, un afflux de vie vient multiplier la puissance d'agir, on se croit irrésistible en vertu d'une aide divine qui garantit contre la défaite et la mort. La guerre est facile alors et aimée bassement.

53. Mais chez la plupart cet état ne dure pas. Un jour vient où la peur, la défaite, la mort des compagnons chéris font plier l'âme du combattant sous la nécessité. La guerre cesse alors d'être un jeu ou un rêve; le guerrier comprend enfin qu'elle existe réellement. C'est une

réalité dure, infiniment trop dure pour pouvoir être supportée, car elle enferme la mort. La pensée de la mort ne peut pas être soutenue, sinon par éclairs, dès qu'on sent que la mort est en effet possible. Il est vrai que tout homme est destiné à mourir, et qu'un soldat peut vieillir parmi les combats; mais pour ceux dont l'âme est soumise au joug de la guerre, le rapport entre la mort et l'avenir n'est pas le même que pour les autres hommes. Pour les autres, la mort est une limite imposée d'avance à l'avenir; pour eux, elle est l'avenir même, l'avenir que leur assigne leur profession. Que des hommes aient pour avenir la mort, cela est contre nature. Dès que la pratique de la guerre a rendu sensible la possibilité de mort qu'enferme chaque minute, la pensée devient incapable de passer d'un jour à son lendemain sans traverser l'image de la mort. L'esprit est alors tendu comme il ne peut souffrir de l'être que peu de temps; mais chaque aube nouvelle amène la même nécessité; les jours ajoutés aux jours font des années. L'âme souffre violence tous les jours. Chaque matin l'âme se mutile de toute aspiration, parce que la pensée ne peut pas voyager dans le temps sans passer par la mort. Ainsi la guerre efface toute idée de but, même l'idée des buts de la guerre. Elle efface la pensée même de mettre fin à la guerre. La possibilité d'une situation si violente est inconcevable tant qu'on n'y est pas; la fin en est inconcevable quand on y est. Ainsi l'on ne fait rien pour amener cette fin. Les bras ne peuvent pas cesser de tenir et de manier les armes en présence d'un ennemi armé; l'esprit devrait combiner pour trouver une issue; il a perdu toute capacité de rien combiner à cet effet. Il est occupé tout entier à se faire violence. Toujours parmi les hommes, qu'il s'agisse de servitude ou de guerre, les malheurs intolérables durent par leur propre poids et semblent ainsi du dehors faciles à porter; ils durent parce qu'ils ôtent les ressources nécessaires pour en sortir.

54. Néanmoins l'âme soumise à la guerre crie vers la délivrance; mais la délivrance même lui apparaît sous une forme tragique, extrême, sous la forme de la destruction. Une fin modérée, raisonnable, laisserait à nu pour la pensée un malheur si violent qu'il ne peut être soutenu même comme souvenir. La terreur, la douleur, l'épuisement, les massacres, les compagnons détruits, on ne croit pas que toutes ces choses puissent cesser de mordre l'âme si l'ivresse de la force n'est venue les noyer. L'idée qu'un effort sans limites pourrait n'avoir apporté qu'un profit nul ou limité fait mal.

Quoi? Laissera-t-on Priam, les Troyens, se vanter

De l'Argienne Hélène, elle pour qui tant de Grecs
Devant Troie ont péri loin de la terre natale?...

Quoi? Tu désires que la cité de Troie aux larges rues,
Nous la laissions, pour qui nous avons souffert tant de misères?

2.176–78, 14.88–89

55. Qu'importe Hélène à Ulysse? Qu'importe même Troie, pleine
de richesses qui ne compenseront pas la ruine d'Ithaque? Troie et
Hélène importent seulement comme causes du sang et des larmes des
Grecs; c'est en s'en rendant maître qu'on peut se rendre maître de
souvenirs affreux. L'âme que l'existence d'un ennemi a contrainte de
détruire en soi ce qu'y avait mis la nature ne croit pouvoir se guérir
que par la destruction de l'ennemi. En même temps, la mort des compagnons bien-aimés suscite une sombre émulation de mourir:

Ah! mourir tout de suite, si mon ami a dû
Succomber sans mon aide! Bien loin de la patrie
Il a péri, et il ne m'a pas eu pour écarter la mort ....
Maintenant je pars pour retrouver le meurtrier d'une tête si chère,
Hector; la mort, je la recevrai au moment où
Zeus voudra l'accomplir, et tous les autres dieux.

18.98–100, 114–16

56. Le même désespoir alors pousse à périr et à tuer:

Je le sais bien, que mon destin est de périr ici,
Loin de mon père et de ma mère aimés; mais cependant
Je ne cesserai que les Troyens n'aient eu leur soûl de guerre.

19.421–23

57. L'homme habité par ce double besoin de mort appartient, tant
qu'il n'est pas devenu autre, à une race différente de la race des vivants.

58. Quel écho peut trouver dans de tels cœurs la timide aspiration
de la vie, quand le vaincu supplie qu'on lui permette de voir encore le
jour? Déjà la possession des armes d'un côté, la privation des armes
de l'autre, ôtent à une vie menacée presque toute importance; et
comment celui qui a détruit en lui-même la pensée que voir la lumière
est doux la respecterait-il dans cette plainte humble et vaine?

Je suis à tes genoux, Achille; aie égard à moi, aie pitié;
Je suis là comme un suppliant, ô fils de Zeus, digne d'égard.
Car chez toi le premier j'ai mangé pain de Déméter,
Ce jour où tu m'as pris dans mon verger bien cultivé.
Et tu m'as vendu, m'envoyant loin de mon père et des miens,

À Lemnos sainte; on t'a donné pour moi une hécatombe.
Je fus racheté pour trois fois plus; cette aurore est pour moi
Aujourd'hui la douzième, depuis que je suis revenu dans Ilion,
Après tant de douleurs. Me voici encore entre tes mains
Par un destin funeste. Je dois être odieux à Zeus le père
Qui de nouveau me livre à toi; pour peu de vie ma mère
M'a enfanté, Laothoè, fille du vieillard Altos ....

21.74–85

59. Quelle réponse accueille ce faible espoir!

Allons, ami, meurs aussi, toi! Pourquoi te plains-tu tellement?
Il est mort aussi, Patrocle, et il valait bien mieux que toi.
Et moi, ne vois-tu pas comme je suis beau et grand?
Je suis de noble race, une déesse est ma mère;
Mais aussi sur moi sont la mort et la dure destinée.
Ce sera l'aurore, ou le soir, ou le milieu du jour,
Lorsqu'à moi aussi par les armes on arrachera la vie ....

21.106–12

60. Il faut, pour respecter la vie en autrui quand on a dû se mutiler soi-même de toute aspiration à vivre, un effort de générosité à briser le cœur. On ne peut supposer aucun des guerriers d'Homère capable d'un tel effort, sinon peut-être celui qui d'une certaine manière se trouve au centre du poème, Patrocle, qui "sut être doux envers tous," et dans l'*Iliade* ne commet rien de brutal ou de cruel. Mais combien connaissons-nous d'hommes, en plusieurs milliers d'années d'histoire, qui aient fait preuve d'une si divine générosité? Il est douteux qu'on puisse en nommer deux ou trois. Faute de cette générosité, le soldat vainqueur est comme un fléau de la nature; possédé par la guerre, il est autant que l'esclave, bien que d'une manière tout autre, devenu une chose, et les paroles sont sans pouvoir sur lui comme sur la matière. L'un et l'autre, au contact de la force, en subissent l'effet infaillible, qui est de rendre ceux qu'elle touche ou muets ou sourds.

61. Telle est la nature de la force. Le pouvoir qu'elle possède de transformer les hommes en choses est double et s'exerce de deux côtés; elle pétrifie différemment, mais également, les âmes de ceux qui la subissent et de ceux qui la manient. Cette propriété atteint le plus haut degré au milieu des armes, à partir du moment où une bataille s'oriente vers une décision. Les batailles ne se décident pas entre hommes qui calculent, combinent, prennent une résolution et l'exécutent, mais entre hommes dépouillés de ces facultés, transformés, tombés au rang soit de la matière inerte qui n'est que passivité,

soit des forces aveugles qui ne sont qu'élan. C'est là le dernier secret de la guerre, et l'*Iliade* l'exprime par ses comparaisons, où les guerriers apparaissent comme les semblables soit de l'incendie, de l'inondation, du vent, des bêtes féroces, de n'importe quelle cause aveugle de désastre, soit des animaux peureux, des arbres, de l'eau, du sable, de tout ce qui est mû par la violence des forces extérieures. Grecs et Troyens, d'un jour à l'autre, parfois d'une heure à l'autre, subissent tour à tour l'une et l'autre transmutation:

> Comme par un lion qui veut tuer des vaches sont assaillies
> Qui dans une prairie marécageuse et vaste paissent
> Par milliers …;
> … toutes elles tremblent; ainsi alors les Achéens
> Avec panique furent mis en fuite par Hector et par Zeus le père,
> Tous ….

> Comme lorsque le feu destructeur tombe sur l'épaisseur d'un bois;
> Partout en tournoyant le vent le porte; alors les fûts,
> Arrachés, tombent sous la pression du feu violent;
> Ainsi l'Atride Agamemnon faisait tomber les têtes
> Des Troyens qui fuyaient ….

15.630–32, 636–38; 11.155–59

62. L'art de la guerre n'est que l'art de provoquer de telles transformations, et le matériel, les procédés, la mort même infligée à l'ennemi ne sont que des moyens à cet effet; il a pour véritable objet l'âme même des combattants. Mais ces transformations constituent toujours un mystère, et les dieux en sont les auteurs, eux qui touchent l'imagination des hommes. Quoi qu'il en soit, cette double propriété de pétrification est essentielle à la force, et une âme placée au contact de la force n'y échappe que par une espèce de miracle. De tels miracles sont rares et courts.

63. La légèreté de ceux qui manient sans respect les hommes et les choses qu'ils ont ou croient avoir à leur merci, le désespoir qui contraint le soldat à détruire, l'écrasement de l'esclave et du vaincu, les massacres, tout contribue à faire un tableau uniforme d'horreur. La force en est le seul héros. Il en résulterait une morne monotonie, s'il n'y avait, parsemés çà et là, des moments lumineux; moments brefs et divins où les hommes ont une âme. L'âme qui s'éveille ainsi, un instant, pour se perdre bientôt après par l'empire de la force, s'éveille pure et intacte; il n'y apparaît aucun sentiment ambigu, compliqué ou trouble; seuls le courage et l'amour y ont place. Parfois un homme

trouve ainsi son âme en délibérant avec lui-même, quand il s'essaye, comme Hector devant Troie, sans secours des dieux ou des hommes, à faire tout seul face au destin. Les autres moments où les hommes trouvent leur âme sont ceux où ils aiment; presque aucune forme pure de l'amour entre les hommes n'est absente de l'*Iliade*.

64. La tradition de l'hospitalité, même après plusieurs générations, l'emporte sur l'aveuglement du combat:

> Ainsi je suis pour toi un hôte aimé au sein d'Argos …
> Évitons les lances l'un de l'autre, et même dans la mêlée.
>
> 6.224–26

65. L'amour du fils pour les parents, du père, de la mère pour le fils, est sans cesse indiqué d'une manière aussi brève que touchante:

> Elle répondit, Thétis, en répandant des larmes:
> "Tu m'es né pour une courte vie, mon enfant, comme tu parles …."
>
> 18.94–95

66. De même l'amour fraternel:

> Mes trois frères, que m'avait enfantés une seule mère,
> Si chéris ….
>
> 19.293–94

67. L'amour conjugal, condamné au malheur, est d'une pureté surprenante. L'époux, en évoquant les humiliations de l'esclavage qui attendent la femme aimée, omet celle dont la seule pensée souillerait d'avance leur tendresse. Rien n'est si simple que les paroles adressées par l'épouse à celui qui va mourir:

> … Il vaudrait mieux pour moi,
> Si je te perds, être sous terre; je n'aurai plus
> D'autre recours, quand tu auras rencontré ton destin,
> Rien que des maux ….
>
> 6.410–13

68. Non moins touchantes sont les paroles adressées à l'époux mort:

> Mon époux, tu es mort avant l'âge, si jeune; et moi, ta veuve,
> Tu me laisses seule dans ma maison; notre enfant encore tout petit
> Que nous avons eu toi et moi, malheureux. Et je ne pense pas
> Que jamais il soit grand ….
> Car tu ne m'as pas en mourant de ton lit tendu les mains,
> Tu n'as pas dit une sage parole, pour que toujours

J'y pense jour et nuit en répandant des larmes.

24.725–28, 743–45

69. La plus belle amitié, celle entre compagnons de combats, fait le thème des derniers chants:

> ... Mais Achille
> Pleurait, songeant au compagnon bien-aimé; le sommeil
> Ne le prit pas, qui dompte tout; il se retournait çà et là ....

24.3–5

70. Mais le triomphe le plus pur de l'amour, la grâce suprême des guerres, c'est l'amitié qui monte au cœur des ennemis mortels. Elle fait disparaître la faim de vengeance pour le fils tué, pour l'ami tué, elle efface par un miracle encore plus grand la distance entre bienfaiteur et suppliant, entre vainqueur et vaincu:

> Mais quand le désir de boire et de manger fut apaisé,
> Alors le Dardanien Priam se prit à admirer Achille,
> Combien il était grand et beau; il avait le visage d'un dieu.
> Et à son tour le Dardanien Priam fut admiré d'Achille
> Qui regardait son beau visage et qui écoutait sa parole.
> Et lorsqu'ils se furent rassasiés de s'être contemplés l'un l'autre ....

24.628–33

71. Ces moments de grâce sont rares dans l'*Iliade*, mais ils suffisent pour faire sentir avec un extrême regret ce que la violence fait et fera périr.

72. Pourtant une telle accumulation de violences serait froide sans un accent d'inguérissable amertume qui se fait continuellement sentir, bien qu'indiqué souvent par un seul mot, souvent même par une coupe de vers, par un rejet. C'est par là que l'*Iliade* est une chose unique, par cette amertume qui procède de la tendresse, et qui s'étend sur tous les humains, égale comme la clarté du soleil. Jamais le ton ne cesse d'être imprégné d'amertume, jamais non plus il ne s'abaisse à la plainte. La justice et l'amour, qui ne peuvent guère avoir de place dans ce tableau d'extrêmes et d'injustes violences, le baignent de leur lumière sans jamais être sensibles autrement que par l'accent. Rien de précieux, destiné ou non à périr, n'est méprisé; la misère de tous est exposée sans dissimulation ni dédain; aucun homme n'est placé au-dessus ou au-dessous de la condition commune à tous les hommes; tout ce qui est détruit est regretté. Vainqueurs et vaincus sont également proches, sont au même titre les semblables du poète et de

l'auditeur. S'il y a une différence, c'est que le malheur des ennemis est peut-être ressenti plus douloureusement.

> Ainsi il tomba là, endormi par un sommeil d'airain,
> Le malheureux, loin de son épouse, en défendant les siens ....
>
> 11.241–42

73. Quel accent pour évoquer le sort de l'adolescent vendu par Achille à Lemnos!

> Onze jours il réjouit son cœur parmi ceux qu'il aimait,
> Revenant de Lemnos; le douzième de nouveau
> Aux mains d'Achille Dieu l'a livré, lui qui devait
> L'envoyer chez Hadès, quoiqu'il ne voulût pas partir.
>
> 21.45–48

74. Et le sort d'Euphorbe, celui qui n'a vu qu'un seul jour de guerre:

> Le sang trempe ses cheveux à ceux des Grâces pareils ....
>
> 17.51

75. Quand on pleure Hector:

> ... gardien des épouses chastes et des petits enfants
>
> 24.730

ces mots sont assez pour faire apparaître la chasteté souillée par force et les enfants livrés aux armes. La fontaine aux portes de Troie devient un objet de regret poignant, quand Hector la dépasse en courant pour sauver sa vie condamnée :

> Là se trouvaient de larges lavoirs, tout auprès,
> Beaux, tout en pierre, où les vêtements resplendissants
> Étaient lavés par les femmes de Troie et par les filles si belles,
> Auparavant, pendant la paix, avant que ne viennent les Achéens.
> C'est par là qu'ils coururent, fuyant, et l'autre derrière poursuivant.
>
> 22.153–57

76. Toute l'*Iliade* est sous l'ombre du malheur le plus grand qui soit parmi les hommes, la destruction d'une cité. Ce malheur n'apparaîtrait pas plus déchirant si le poète était né à Troie. Mais le ton n'est pas différent quand il s'agit des Achéens qui périssent bien loin de la patrie.

77. Les brèves évocations du monde de la paix font mal, tant cette autre vie, cette vie des vivants, apparaît calme et pleine:

Tant que ce fut l'aurore et que le jour monta,
Des deux côtés les traits portèrent, les hommes tombèrent.
Mais à l'heure, même où le bûcheron va préparer son repas
Dans les vallons des montagnes, lorsque ses bras sont rassasiés
De couper les grands arbres, et qu'un dégoût lui monte au cœur,
Et que le désir de la douce nourriture le saisit aux entrailles,
À cette heure, par leur valeur, les Danaens rompirent le front.

11.84–90

78. Tout ce qui est absent de la guerre, tout ce que la guerre détruit ou menace est enveloppé de poésie dans l'*Iliade*; les faits de guerre ne le sont jamais. Le passage de la vie à la mort n'est voilé par aucune réticence:

Alors sautèrent ses dents; il vint des deux côtés
Du sang aux yeux; le sang que par les lèvres et les narines
Il rendait bouche ouverte; la mort de son noir nuage l'enveloppa.

16.348–50

79. La froide brutalité des faits de guerre n'est déguisée par rien, parce que ni vainqueurs ni vaincus ne sont admirés, méprisés ni haïs. Le destin et les dieux décident presque toujours du sort changeant des combats. Dans les limites assignées par le destin, les dieux disposent souverainement de la victoire et de la défaite; c'est toujours eux qui provoquent les folies et les trahisons par lesquelles la paix est chaque fois empêchée; la guerre est leur affaire propre, et ils n'ont pour mobiles que le caprice et la malice. Quant aux guerriers, les comparaisons qui les font apparaître, vainqueurs ou vaincus, comme des bêtes ou des choses ne peuvent faire éprouver ni admiration ni mépris, mais seulement le regret que les hommes puissent être ainsi transformés.

80. L'extraordinaire équité qui inspire l'*Iliade* a peut-être des exemples inconnus de nous, mais n'a pas eu d'imitateurs. C'est à peine si l'on sent que le poète est grec et non troyen. Le ton du poème semble porter directement témoignage de l'origine des parties les plus anciennes; l'histoire ne nous donnera peut-être jamais là-dessus de clarté. Si l'on croit avec Thucydide que, quatre-vingts ans après la destruction de Troie, les Achéens souffrirent à leur tour une conquête, on peut se demander si ces chants, où le fer n'est que rarement nommé, ne sont pas des chants de ces vaincus dont certains peut-être s'exilèrent. Contraints de vivre et de mourir "bien loin de la patrie" comme les Grecs tombés devant Troie, ayant comme les Troyens

perdu leurs cités, ils se retrouvaient eux-mêmes aussi bien dans les vainqueurs, qui étaient leurs pères, que dans les vaincus, dont la misère ressemblait à la leur; la vérité de cette guerre encore proche pouvait leur apparaître à travers les années, n'étant voilée ni par l'ivresse de l'orgueil ni par l'humiliation. Ils pouvaient se la représenter à la fois en vaincus et en vainqueurs, et connaître ainsi ce que jamais vainqueurs ni vaincus n'ont connu, étant les uns et les autres aveuglés. Ce n'est là qu'un rêve; on ne peut guère que rêver sur des temps si lointains.

81. Quoi qu'il en soit, ce poème est une chose miraculeuse. L'amertume y porte sur la seule juste cause d'amertume, la subordination de l'âme humaine à la force, c'est-à-dire, en fin de compte, à la matière. Cette subordination est la même chez tous les mortels, quoique l'âme la porte diversement selon le degré de vertu. Nul dans l'*Iliade* n'y est soustrait, de même que nul n'y est soustrait sur terre. Nul de ceux qui y succombent n'est regardé de ce fait comme méprisable. Tout ce qui, à l'intérieur de l'âme et dans les relations humaines, échappe à l'empire de la force est aimé, mais aimé douloureusement, à cause du danger de destruction continuellement suspendu. Tel est l'esprit de la seule épopée véritable que possède l'Occident. L'*Odyssée* semble n'être qu'une excellente imitation, tantôt de l'*Iliade*, tantôt de poèmes orientaux; l'*Énéide* est une imitation qui, si brillante qu'elle soit, est déparée par la froideur, la déclamation et le mauvais goût. Les chansons de geste n'ont pas su atteindre la grandeur faute d'équité; la mort d'un ennemi n'est pas ressentie par l'auteur et le lecteur, dans la *Chanson de Roland*, comme la mort de Roland.

82. La tragédie attique, du moins celle d'Eschyle et de Sophocle, est la vraie continuation de l'épopée. La pensée de la justice l'éclaire sans jamais y intervenir; la force y apparaît dans sa froide dureté, toujours accompagnée des effets funestes auxquels n'échappe ni celui qui en use ni celui qui la souffre; l'humiliation de l'âme sous la contrainte n'y est ni déguisée, ni enveloppée de pitié facile, ni proposée au mépris; plus d'un être blessé par la dégradation du malheur y est offert à l'admiration. L'Évangile est la dernière et merveilleuse expression du génie grec, comme l'*Iliade* en est la première; l'esprit de la Grèce s'y laisse voir non seulement en ce qu'il y est ordonné de rechercher à l'exclusion de tout autre bien "le royaume et la justice de notre Père céleste," mais aussi en ce que la misère humaine y est exposée, et cela

chez un être divin en même temps qu'humain. Les récits de la Passion montrent qu'un esprit divin, uni à la chair, est altéré par le malheur, tremble devant la souffrance et la mort, se sent, au fond de la détresse, séparé des hommes et de Dieu. Le sentiment de la misère humaine leur donne cet accent de simplicité qui est la marque du génie grec, et qui fait tout le prix de la tragédie attique et de l'*Iliade*. Certaines paroles rendent un son étrangement voisin de celui de l'épopée, et l'adolescent troyen envoyé chez Hadès, quoiqu'il ne voulût pas partir, vient à la mémoire quand le Christ dit à Pierre: "Un autre te ceindra et te mènera où tu ne veux pas aller." Cet accent n'est pas séparable de la pensée qui inspire l'Évangile; car le sentiment de la misère humaine est une condition de la justice et de l'amour. Celui qui ignore à quel point la fortune variable et la nécessité tiennent toute âme humaine sous leur dépendance ne peut pas regarder comme des semblables ni aimer comme soi-même ceux que le hasard a séparés de lui par un abîme. La diversité des contraintes qui pèsent sur les hommes fait naître l'illusion qu'il y a parmi eux des espèces distinctes qui ne peuvent communiquer. Il n'est possible d'aimer et d'être juste que si l'on connaît l'empire de la force et si l'on sait ne pas le respecter.

83. Les rapports de l'âme humaine et du destin, dans quelle mesure chaque âme modèle son propre sort, ce qu'une impitoyable nécessité transforme dans une âme quelle qu'elle soit au gré du sort variable, ce qui par l'effet de la vertu et de la grâce peut rester intact, c'est une matière où le mensonge est facile et séduisant. L'orgueil, l'humiliation, la haine, le mépris, l'indifférence, le désir d'oublier ou d'ignorer, tout contribue à en donner la tentation. En particulier, rien n'est plus rare qu'une juste expression du malheur; en le peignant, on feint presque toujours de croire tantôt que la déchéance est une vocation innée du malheureux, tantôt qu'une âme peut porter le malheur sans en recevoir la marque, sans qu'il change toutes les pensées d'une manière qui n'appartient qu'à lui. Les Grecs, le plus souvent, eurent la force d'âme qui permet de ne pas se mentir; ils en furent récompensés et surent atteindre en toute chose le plus haut degré de lucidité, de pureté et de simplicité. Mais l'esprit qui s'est transmis de l'*Iliade* à l'Évangile en passant par les penseurs et les poètes tragiques n'a guère franchi les limites de la civilisation grecque; et depuis qu'on a détruit la Grèce il n'en est resté que des reflets.

84. Les Romains et les Hébreux se sont crus les uns et les autres

soustraits à la commune misère humaine, les premiers en tant que nation choisie par le destin pour être la maîtresse du monde, les seconds par la faveur de leur Dieu et dans la mesure exacte où ils lui obéissaient. Les Romains méprisaient les étrangers, les ennemis, les vaincus, leurs sujets, leurs esclaves; aussi n'ont-ils eu ni épopées ni tragédies. Ils remplaçaient les tragédies par les jeux de gladiateurs. Les Hébreux voyaient dans le malheur le signe du péché et par suite un motif légitime de mépris; ils regardaient leurs ennemis vaincus comme étant en horreur à Dieu même et condamnés à expier des crimes, ce qui rendait la cruauté permise et même indispensable. Aussi aucun texte de l'Ancien Testament ne rend-il un son comparable à celui de l'épopée grecque, sinon peut-être certaines parties du poème de Job. Romains et Hébreux ont été admirés, lus, imités dans les actes et les paroles, cités toutes les fois qu'il y avait lieu de justifier un crime, pendant vingt siècles de christianisme.

85. De plus l'esprit de l'Évangile ne s'est pas transmis pur aux générations successives de chrétiens. Dès les premiers temps on a cru voir un signe de la grâce, chez les martyrs, dans le fait de subir les souffrances et la mort avec joie; comme si les effets de la grâce pouvaient aller plus loin chez les hommes que chez le Christ. Ceux qui pensent que Dieu lui-même, une fois devenu homme, n'a pu avoir devant les yeux la rigueur du destin sans en trembler d'angoisse, auraient dû comprendre que seuls peuvent s'élever en apparence au-dessus de la misère humaine les hommes qui déguisent la rigueur du destin à leurs propres yeux, par le secours de l'illusion, de l'ivresse ou du fanatisme. L'homme qui n'est pas protégé par l'armure d'un mensonge ne peut souffrir la force sans en être atteint jusqu'à l'âme. La grâce peut empêcher que cette atteinte le corrompe, mais elle ne peut pas empêcher la blessure. Pour l'avoir trop oublié, la tradition chrétienne n'a su retrouver que très rarement la simplicité qui rend poignante chaque phrase des récits de la Passion. D'autre part, la coutume de convertir par contrainte a voilé les effets de la force sur l'âme de ceux qui la manient.

86. Malgré la brève ivresse causée lors de la Renaissance par la découverte des lettres grecques, le génie de la Grèce n'a pas ressuscité au cours de vingt siècles. Il en apparaît quelque chose dans Villon, Shakespeare, Cervantès, Molière, et une fois dans Racine. La misère humaine est mise à nu, à propos de l'amour, dans *L'École des Femmes*, dans *Phèdre*; étrange siècle d'ailleurs, où, au contraire de l'âge épique,

il n'était permis d'apercevoir la misère de l'homme que dans l'amour, au lieu que les effets de la force dans la guerre et dans la politique devaient toujours être enveloppés de gloire. On pourrait peut-être citer encore d'autres noms. Mais rien de ce qu'ont produit les peuples d'Europe ne vaut le premier poème connu qui soit apparu chez l'un d'eux. Ils retrouveront peut-être le génie épique quand ils sauront ne rien croire à l'abri du sort, ne jamais admirer la force, ne pas haïr les ennemis et ne pas mépriser les malheureux. Il est douteux que ce soit pour bientôt.

PART III

The *Iliad* or the Poem of Force

1. The true hero, the true subject matter, the center of the *Iliad* is force. The force that men wield, the force that subdues men, in the face of which human flesh shrinks back. The human soul seems ever conditioned by its ties with force, swept away, blinded by the force it believes it can control, bowed under the constraint of the force it submits to. Those who have supposed that force, thanks to progress, now belongs to the past, have seen a record of that in Homer's poem; those wise enough to discern the force at the center of all human history, today as in the past, find in the *Iliad* the most beautiful and flawless of mirrors.

2. Force is that which makes a thing of whoever submits to it. Exercised to the extreme, it makes the human being a thing quite literally, that is, a dead body. Someone was there and, the next moment, no one. The *Iliad* never tires of presenting us this tableau:

> ... the horses
> made the swift chariots thunder along the paths of war
> in mourning for their blameless drivers. On the earth
> they lie, much dearer to the vultures than to their wives.

> 11.159–62

3. The hero is a thing dragged in the dust behind a chariot:

> ... All around, the black hair
> was spread, and the whole head lay in the dust,
> just before so charming; now Zeus has granted
> to his enemies to debase it on his native land.

> 22.401–4

4. We taste the bitterness of such a tableau undiluted, mitigated by no comforting lie, no consoling expectation of immortality, no faded nimbus of glory or patriotism.

> His soul flies from his limbs, goes to Hades,
> grieving its destiny, relinquishing its strength and youth.
>
> 22.362–63

5. Still more moving and painfully contrastive is the sudden evoking and immediate effacing of another world, the distant, fragile, touching world of peace, of the family, a world where each man means more than anything to those around him.

> She called to her fair-haired servants in the house
> to put by the fire a large tripod, in order that there might be
> a warm bath for Hector on his return from combat.
> So naive! She knew not that far indeed from warm baths
> Achilles' arm had beaten him down, because of green-eyed Athena.
>
> 22.442–46

6. Truly, he was far from warm baths, that hapless man. Nor was he alone. Nearly all of the *Iliad* takes place far from warm baths. Nearly all human life has always taken place far from warm baths.

7. The force that kills is summary and crude. How much more varied in operation, how much more stunning in effect is that other sort of force, that which does not kill, or rather does not kill just yet. It will kill for a certainty, or it will kill perhaps, or it may merely hang over the being it can kill at any instant; in all cases, it changes the human being into stone. From the power to change a human being into a thing by making him die there comes another power, in its way more momentous, that of making a still living human being into a thing. He is living, he has a soul; he is nonetheless a thing. Strange being—a thing with a soul; strange situation for the soul! Who can say how it must each moment conform itself, twist and contort itself? It was not created to inhabit a thing; when it compels itself to do so, it endures violence through and through.

8. A man disarmed and exposed, toward whom a weapon points, becomes a corpse before being touched. For one last moment, he calculates, acts, hopes:

> Immobile, he reflected. The other approached, terrified,
> eager to grasp his knees. He longed in his heart
> to escape evil death, dark destiny ....
> With one arm he grasped his knees in supplication

with the other he held and would not let go the sharp spear....

21.64–66, 71–72

9. But before long he understands that the weapon will not turn aside, and, though breathing still, he is no more than matter; still thinking, he can think no more:

> So spoke this splendid son of Priam
> in suppliant words. He heard a pitiless response ....
> He [Achilles] spoke; his knees and heart failed the other;
> he let go the spear and fell back, stretched forth
> both hands. Achilles drew his sharp sword,
> struck him at the collarbone along the neck; and full length
> plunged in the two-edged sword. Face down on the ground,
> he lay sprawled, and the black blood flowed, staining the earth.

21.97–98, 114–19

10. When, outside of combat, a weak and unarmed stranger supplicates a warrior, he is not automatically condemned to death; but an instant of impatience on the warrior's part is sufficient to strip him of his life. It is enough for his flesh to lose the chief quality of living flesh. A bit of living flesh exhibits vitality above all by reflex action; a frog's leg, under electric shock, twitches; the closeness or touch of a horrifying or terrible thing makes any bundle of flesh, nerves, and muscles twitch. Only the suppliant does not tremble or shiver; he has not the license; his lips proceed to touch the object for him most charged with horror:

> No one saw the great Priam come in. He stopped,
> grasped Achilles' knees, kissed his hands,
> terrible, manslaughtering, which had slain so many of his sons.

24.477–79

11. The spectacle of a human being reduced to this degree of misery chills one like the sight of a dead body.

> As when hard misery seizes someone when in his own land
> he has murdered, and when he arrives at the home of another,
> some rich man; a shiver seizes those who look at him;
> so Achilles shivered seeing the godlike Priam.
> The others too shivered looking at one another.

24.480–84

12. But this is momentary, and soon the very presence of the miserable one is forgotten:

He spoke. The other, thinking of his father, desired to weep;
Taking him by the arm, he pushed the old man away a little.
Both were remembering, one Hector slayer of men,
and he huddled in tears at Achilles' feet, against the earth;
but Achilles wept for his father and then too for
Patroclus; their sobbing filled the hut.

24.507–12

13. Not through insensitivity does Achilles push to the ground the old man clutching his knees; the words of Priam, calling to Achilles' mind his own old father, have moved him to tears. He simply finds himself as uninhibited in his attitudes and actions as if, instead of a suppliant, an inanimate object had touched his knees. The human beings around us have by their very presence a power, belonging only to them, to stop, to inhibit, to alter each action our body traces; a passer-by does not deflect us from our path in the same way as a billboard; one does not rise, walk, or sit when alone in one's own room the same as when one has a visitor. But this indefinable influence of the human presence is not exerted by those whom a moment of impatience may rend from life before even a thought has time to condemn them to death. Before them, others move about as if they were not there; and they for their part, in danger of being reduced to nothing in an instant, imitate nonentity. Pushed, they fall; fallen, they lie on the ground, so long as chance does not prompt someone to raise them up. But even when at length they are raised up, addressed with kind words, it does not occur to them to take this resurrection seriously, to dare to express a wish; an irritated voice may return them instantly to silence:

He spoke, and the old man quaked and submitted.

24.571

14. At least some suppliants, once granted their wish, become again men like others. But there are still more miserable beings who, without dying, have become things for life. In their days there is no play, no space, no opening for anything that comes from within. These are not men living harder lives than others, or socially inferior to others; they are an alternative human species, a hybrid of man and corpse. That a human being should be a thing is a logical contradiction; but when the impossible has become a reality, the contradiction lacerates the soul. This thing aspires at all times to be a man or a woman, and never attains the goal. This is a death that extends

throughout a life, a life that death has frozen long before putting an end to it.

15. The maiden, daughter of a priest, will suffer this fate:

> I will not return her. Before that old age will seize her,
> in my home, in Argos, far from her homeland,
> moving along the loom and lying in my bed.

1.29–31

16. The young woman, the young mother, wife of the prince, will suffer it:

> And perhaps one day in Argos you will weave fabric for another
> and you will carry the water from the spring Messeis or Hypereia,
> despite yourself, under the compulsion of hard necessity.

6.456–58

17. The infant heir of the royal scepter will undergo it:

> Those women no doubt will go in the hold of the hollow ships,
> myself among them; you, my child, either along with me
> you will follow and perform degrading labor,
> toiling under the eyes of a pitiless master ....

24.731–34

18. In the eyes of a mother, such a destiny is more awful for her child than death itself; the husband hopes to die before seeing his wife reduced to it; the father calls all the plagues of the heavens down on the army that subjects his daughter to it. But so brutal a destiny nullifies the curses, the rebellions, the comparisons, the thoughts of the future and the past, almost the memories of those it has befallen. It is not the part of the slave to be faithful to his city and his dead.

19. When one of those suffers or dies who have made him lose everything, who have sacked his town, massacred his people before his eyes, only then does the slave weep. Naturally, for only then are tears permitted him, even required of him. But in slavery, are not tears ready to flow as soon as they may do so with impunity?

> She spoke weeping, and the women wailed,
> taking Patroclus as pretext each for her own anguish.

19.301–2

20. At no time may the slave express anything except what is pleasing to his master. This is why, in a life so bleak, no emotion can germinate and animate him a bit except love of the master; every

other path is barred to the gift of love, just as for a harnessed horse, the shafts, the reins, the bits bar all roads save one. And if by some miracle there appears the hope of becoming someone one day, by some favor, to what lengths will they not go in thankfulness and love for those very men against whom the recent past should inspire revulsion:

> My husband, to whom my honored father and mother gave me,
> I have seen before my city stabbed by the sharp bronze.
> My three brothers, whom a sole mother bore with me,
> so beloved! they have found their fated day.
> But you did not let me, when my husband was slain by swift Achilles,
> and the holy city of Mynes was sacked,
> you did not let me shed tears; you promised me that godlike Achilles
> would take me for his wedded wife and would take me in his ships
> to Phthia, to be married among the Myrmidons.
> So unceasingly I bewail you, you who were always so sweet.
>
> 19.291–300

21. No one can lose more than the slave loses; he loses his entire inner life. He may regain a bit of it only when there seems to be a chance to alter his fate. Such is the realm of force: this realm extends as far as that of nature. Nature also, when essential needs come into play, effaces inner life and even the grief of a mother:

> Since even Niobe of the lovely locks thought to eat,
> she whose twelve children perished in her home,
> six sons and six daughters in the bloom of their youth.
> Apollo slew the boys with his silver bow
> in his wrath against Niobe; Artemis who loves the arrows slew the maidens.
> All because she had likened herself to fair-cheeked Leto,
> saying "she has two children; I, I have borne many."
> And those two, though they were only two, had made all the others die.
> Nine days they lay in death; no one came
> to bury them. The people had become stones by the will of Zeus.
> And on the tenth day, they were buried by the gods of heaven.
> But she thought to eat, when she grew tired of tears.
>
> 24.602–13

22. No one has ever described with such bitterness the misery of man, which renders him unable even to comprehend his misery.

23. Force wielded by others dominates the soul like an excessive hunger, since it comprises an unending power of life and death. And it is a realm as cold and harsh as if it were governed by inert matter.

The man who finds himself on all sides the weaker is solitary even in the heart of cities, more solitary even than the man lost in a desert.

> Two urns are positioned at the threshold of Zeus,
> where are held the gifts he grants, the one sort bad, the other good....
> The one on whom he bestows deadly gifts he subjects to insults;
> a fearful need hunts him across the divine earth;
> He wanders and gets the respect of neither men nor gods.
>
> 24.527–28, 531–33

24. As pitilessly as force annihilates, equally without pity it intoxicates those who possess or believe they possess it. In reality, no one possesses it. People in the *Iliad* are not segregated into conquered, slaves, suppliants on the one side and conquerors and masters on the other; every human being may at any moment be compelled to submit to force. The warriors, though free and armed, submit no less to commands and insults:

> Every man of the host whom he saw and caught shouting,
> he struck with his scepter and scolded thus:
> "Wretch, hold your tongue, listen to others speaking,
> your betters. You're neither brave nor strong,
> you're worthless in battle, worthless in the council."
>
> 2.198–202

25. Thersites pays dearly for his very sensible words, words just like those Achilles speaks.

> He struck him; he buckled, his tears sprang forth,
> a bloody bruise formed on his back
> under the golden scepter; he sat in fear.
> In a sad daze he wiped his tears.
> The others, despite their irritation, laughed and took pleasure at the sight.
>
> 2.266–70

26. Even Achilles, that fierce, invincible hero, is presented to us at the beginning of the poem weeping from humiliation and impotent sorrow, after they have taken away before his very eyes the woman he wanted for a wife, and he dared not oppose it.

> ... But Achilles
> sat weeping, away from his comrades, apart,
> at the edge of the foamy waves, gazing on the wine-dark sea.
>
> 1.348–50

27. Agamemnon has intentionally humbled Achilles to show that he is the superior:

> Thus you will grasp
> that I count for more than you, and all others will think twice
> before treating me as an equal and opposing me.
>
> 1.185–87

28. But a few days later, the supreme chief weeps in his turn, forced to demean himself, to supplicate, and he bears the pain of doing so to no avail.

29. The disgrace of fear spares no warrior. Heroes tremble like the others. A single challenge by Hector is enough to dismay all the Greeks without a single exception, save for Achilles and his men, who are absent:

> He spoke and all were silent and held their peace;
> they were ashamed to refuse, scared to accept.
>
> 7.92–93

30. But as soon as Ajax comes forward, fear changes sides:

> A shudder of fear weakened the limbs of the Trojans;
> the heart of Hector himself leapt in his breast;
> But he was no longer free to shudder or flee.
>
> 7.215–17

31. Two days later, Ajax, in turn, feels terror:

> Father Zeus on high makes fear grow in Ajax.
> He stops, stunned, puts behind him the seven-hide shield,
> and trembling looks all around at the host, like a beast.
>
> 11.544–46

32. A moment of fear and trembling comes to Achilles himself, though, truth be told, before a river, not a mere man. Excluding him, all without exception are shown beaten at some point. Valor contributes less in determining victory than does blind destiny, signified by Zeus's golden scales:

> At this moment Father Zeus used his golden scales.
> He placed in it two fates of all-reaping death,
> one for the horse-breaking Trojans, one for the bronze-clad Greeks.
> As he grasped the scales in the middle, the Greeks' fatal day tipped down.
>
> 8.69–72

33. By virtue of its blindness, destiny institutes a type of justice, blind as well, that exacts from men at arms a punishment in kind; the *Iliad* had formulated that code long before the Gospels, and in almost the same phrases:

Ares is just and kills those who kill.

18.309

34. Though all are destined from birth to endure violence, the realm of circumstances closes their minds to this truth. The strong is never perfectly strong nor the weak perfectly weak, but neither knows this. They believe they are of different species; the weak man does not consider himself like the strong, nor is he regarded as such. He who possesses force moves in a frictionless environment; nothing in the human matter around him puts an interval for reflection between impulse and action. Where reflection has no place, there is neither justice nor forethought: hence the ruthless and mindless behavior of warriors. Their sword plunges into a disarmed opponent at their knees; they vaunt over a dying man, telling him the insults his body will undergo. Achilles cuts the throats of twelve Trojan youths on the pyre of Patroclus as casually as we cut flowers for a grave. In wielding their power they never suspect that the consequences of their actions will afflict them in turn. When one can silence an old man with a word, cause him to tremble and submit, does such a one consider the curses of a priest to be of any consequence in the eyes of soothsayers? Does he forbear to appropriate the woman Achilles loves, knowing that neither has any choice but to submit? When Achilles delights to see the wretched Greeks flee, can he grasp that this flight, which will continue and end at his whim, will cost his friend and even himself their lives? Those to whom fate has loaned force perish through their over-reliance on it.

35. It is impossible that they should not perish, since they neither consider their own force to be limited nor recognize that their relations with others are a balance of unequal forces. Other men do not pause in their actions to have some regard for their fellow man; they conclude that destiny has granted them every license and none to their inferiors. From this point, they overstep the force at their disposal—inevitably, for they fail to see its limits. They are then surrendered ineluctably to chance, and things no longer obey them. Chance sometimes helps, sometimes hurts them; they are exposed

quite naked to sorrow, without the armor of power that had shielded their spirit, with nothing to insulate them any longer from tears.

36. This geometrically stringent chastisement, which spontaneously punishes the abuse of force, was the primary issue in Greek thought. It constitutes the heart and soul of epic; under the name "Nemesis," it is the subject of Aeschylean tragedy; the Pythagoreans, Socrates, Plato move from this starting point to their reflections on man and the cosmos. The concept is familiar wherever the spirit of Greek thought has penetrated. This Greek idea perhaps survives as "karma" in regions of the East pervaded by Buddhism. But the West has lost it, lacking even a word for it in any of its languages. The notions of limit, measure, balance, which should shape the conduct of life, are employed only in a mundane way in the technical sphere. We are geometricians of mere matter; the Greeks were, from the outset, geometricians in the apprenticeship of virtue.

37. The progression of war in the *Iliad* comprises a simple seesaw movement. The victor of the moment feels himself invincible, even though a few brief hours earlier he encountered defeat. He forgets that victory is ephemeral. At the end of the first day of the campaign recounted in the *Iliad*, the victorious Greeks could undoubtedly have gained the object of their efforts, namely Helen and her riches; at least if one imagines, as Homer did, that the Greek army had reason to believe Helen was in Troy. The Egyptian priests, who must have known, stated to Herodotus much later that she was actually to be found in Egypt. At all events, that evening, the Greeks do not want her any more.

> "Let none now accept either the goods of Paris,
> or Helen; even a dolt can see
> that Troy is now on the brink of ruin."
> He spoke, and all among the Achaeans hailed his words.

> 7.400–403

38. They want nothing less than the whole. All the wealth of Troy as booty, all the palaces, the temples, and the houses in ashes; all the women and children slaves; all the men corpses. They forget one detail: that all is not in their power, since they are not in Troy. Maybe they will be there tomorrow, maybe not.

39. Hector has the same lapse of memory that very day:

> Since I know this well in my guts and my heart;
> a day will come when holy Ilion will perish,

and Priam, and the people of Priam of the good spear.
But I think less of the sorrow in store for the Trojans,
and of Hecuba herself, and of king Priam,
and of my brothers who, so many and so brave,
will fall in the dust under the blows of the enemy,
than of you, when one of the bronze-cuirassed Greeks
shall carry you off in tears, stripping you of your freedom....
As for me, may I be dead and the earth have covered me,
ere I hear you cry or see you carried away!

6.447–55, 464–65

40. What wouldn't he give at this moment to avert the horrors he believes unavoidable? But he could only give in vain. Two days afterward, the Greeks have fled wretchedly, and Agamemnon even wants to take to sea again. Hector, who could easily have secured the departure of the Greeks by a small offer, is no longer even willing to permit them to go with empty hands:

Let us burn fires all around and let the glare go heavenward
for fear in the night the long-haired Greeks
escape making a break onto the broad back of the sea....
Let many carry wound marks with them to digest at home ...
so that all the world may shrink from
bringing grief-causing war to the Trojans, breakers of horses.

8.509–11, 513, 515–16

41. His desire is realized; the Greeks remain; and next day, at noon, they make a piteous thing of him and his men:

They fled across the plain like cattle
that a lion, coming on them in the night, chases before him ....
Thus the mighty son of Atreus, Agamemnon, pursued them,
killing without fail the hindmost; they for their part fled.

11.172–73, 177–78

42. In the course of the afternoon, Hector regains the upper hand, retreats again, then routs the Greeks, then is repulsed by Patroclus and his fresh troops. Patroclus, who pursues his advantage beyond his forces, ends up stripped of his armor, wounded, and exposed to Hector's sword. That evening victorious Hector harshly quashes the sensible counsel of Polydamas:

"Now that the devious son of Cronus has granted me
glory by the ships, thrusting the Greeks to the sea,
imbecile! don't propose such counsels before the people.
No Trojan will listen to you; I for my part will not allow it."...

So spoke Hector, and the Trojans shouted assent.

18.293–96, 310

43. The next day Hector is lost. Achilles makes him retreat across the whole plain and goes in for the kill. He has always been the more powerful of the two in battle; how much more so after several weeks of rest, transported by vengeance and victory, facing a worn-out enemy! And there is Hector alone before Troy's walls, utterly alone, awaiting death and trying to brace his soul to face it:

> Alas! if I go behind the gate and the rampart,
> Polydamas will straightaway shame me....
> Now that I have lost my men through folly,
> I fear the Trojans and the Trojan women in their trailing robes,
> and I dread to hear it said by those less brave than I:
> "Hector, overconfident in his strength, has destroyed his country."...
> Yet if I were to put down my curved shield,
> my good helmet, and, leaning my spear on the rampart,
> if I were to go to meet famed Achilles?...
> But why does my heart counsel me such counsels?
> I will not approach him; he would have no pity,
> no respect; he would slay me, if I were thus exposed,
> like a woman....

22.99–100, 104–7, 111–13, 122–25

44. Hector evades none of the pain and shame that befall the luckless. Alone, stripped of all the prestige of force, the courage that kept him outside the walls does not keep him from fleeing:

> Hector, at the sight of him, was seized by trembling. He could not steel himself to stand firm....
> ... It is not for a ewe or an ox hide
> that they struggle, the usual race-prizes;
> it is for a life that they run, that of Hector, breaker of horses.

22.136–37, 159–61

45. Mortally wounded, he enhances the triumph of the conqueror by his futile entreaties:

> I beg you by your life, by your knees, by your parents....

22.338

46. But the audience of the *Iliad* knew that Hector's death would give only fleeting joy to Achilles, and the death of Achilles only fleeting joy to the Trojans, and the annihilation of Troy only fleeting joy to the Achaeans.

47. Thus violence overwhelms those it touches. In the end, it seems as external to the one who wields it as to the one who endures it. Here is born the notion of a destiny under which executioners and their victims are similarly innocent: conquerors and conquered are brothers in the same misery, each a heartache to the other.

> A single son was born to him, born to a short life; and
> he grows older without my attentions, since far from my homeland
> I remain at Troy to work evil against you and your sons.
>
> 24.540–42

48. The tempered use of force, indispensable to the escape from its machinery, would demand superhuman virtue, as rare as steadfast dignity in weakness. Further, moderation itself carries risks, for the prestige that is three-fourths of force consists above all of the magnificent indifference of the strong toward the weak, an indifference so contagious that it infects even those who are its object. But it is not usually political considerations that counsel excess. The temptation to excess is virtually irresistible. Reasonable words are sometimes spoken in the *Iliad*; those of Thersites are reasonable in the highest degree. So, too, are those of the angry Achilles:

> Nothing is worth my life, not even all the goods they say
> Ilion holds, that city so prosperous....
> Because one may take cattle and fat sheep as booty ....
> A human life, however, once lost, cannot be recouped.
>
> 9.401–2, 406, 408

49. But reasonable words fall into the void. If an inferior speaks them, he is punished and silenced; if a superior, he does not abide by them in his actions. And there is always some god to recommend the irrational course. In the end, the very notion that one might want to evade the career allotted one by fate—that of killing and dying—vanishes from the spirit:

> ... we whom Zeus
> has designated for suffering from youth to old age
> in grievous warfare, till we perish to the last man.
>
> 14.85–87

50. These warriors, like those at Craonne much later, sensed that they were "the condemned."

51. They have fallen into this condition through the simplest of snares. At the outset, their heart is light, as always when a force faces

mere void. Their weapons are in their hands; the enemy is absent. Except when one has a spirit downcast by the enemy's reputation, one is always much stronger than an absent opponent, who imposes no yoke of necessity. No necessity appears yet to the spirit of those going forth in this way, as if to a game, a holiday free from daily care.

> What happened to our boasts, used to bolster our brave selves,
> which you at Lemnos made in your vanity,
> gorging yourselves on the meat of straight-horned oxen,
> drinking from cups brimming with wine?
> That each against one or two hundred of these Trojans
> could hold his own in battle: and behold one alone is too much for us!
>
> 8.229–34

52. Even after a first taste of it, war does not instantly cease to seem a game. The necessity proper to war is terrible, another thing altogether from that connected with peace; the soul will submit to it only when it cannot escape it any longer; and, as long as it manages to escape it, it passes days empty of necessity, days of play, of dream, whimsical and illusory. Danger is then an abstraction, and the lives one destroys are like playthings broken by a child and just as inconsequential; heroism is histrionic and besmirched by boasting. If for a moment a surge of energy amplifies the power of action, one feels irresistible, divinely exempted from defeat and death. War is then a lark and vulgarly loved.

53. But for the majority, this situation does not last. A day comes when fear, defeat, the death of beloved comrades make the soul of the warrior succumb to necessity. War then ceases to be a game or a dream; the warrior finally understands that it actually exists. It is a harsh reality, infinitely too harsh to tolerate, for it embraces death. The idea of death is insupportable, except in short bursts, when one knows that death is in fact possible. It is true that every man is destined to die and that a soldier may grow old in battles, but for those whose soul is bent beneath the yoke of war, the connection between death and the future is not the same as for other men. For others, death is a limit imposed on the future. For soldiers, it is the future itself, the future their vocation allots. That men should have death for their future is unnatural. Once the practice of war has made clear the possibility of death contained in every moment, thought becomes incapable of passing from one day to the next without encountering the image of death. The spirit is then strained so much that it can endure

only a short time; but every new dawn brings with it the same necessity; days joined to days fill out years. The soul undergoes duress every day. Each morning it amputates itself of all aspiration, for thought cannot travel in time without encountering death. Thus war expunges every concept of a goal, even the goals of war. It expunges the idea of an end of war. The possibility of a situation so violent is unthinkable outside that situation; an end to it unthinkable within it. Thus, one does nothing to effect this end. One's hands cannot cease to hold and wield weapons in the presence of an armed opponent; the mind should devise a way out but has lost all ability to devise such a thing. It is occupied entirely in violating itself. Always among human beings, as regards slavery or warfare, insufferable agonies persist by their own inertia and appear from outside easy to bear; they persist because they sap the resources needed to escape.

54. None the less, the soul subjected to war cries out for deliverance, but deliverance itself appears under a tragic and extreme guise, the guise of destruction. A moderate, reasonable aim would expose thought to an agony so violent as to be unendurable even in reminiscence. The terror, the grief, the weariness, the massacres, the comrades slain—only the intoxication with force can drown out all these things that rend the soul. The idea that boundless effort should bring little or no gain is painful.

> What's this? Shall we let Priam and the Trojans brag
> of Argive Helen, she for whom so many Greeks
> have died at Troy far from their native soil?...
>
> What's this? Do you want us to leave the city of Troy of the wide ways
> for which we have suffered so many hardships?

> 2.176–78, 14.88–89

55. What, after all, is Helen to Ulysses? What indeed to him is Troy, filled with riches that won't compensate for the ruin of Ithaca? Troy and Helen are important only as causing bloodshed and tears for the Greeks; mastery of Troy and Helen means mastery of fearful memories. When the existence of an enemy has compelled the soul to destroy in itself what nature has put there, that soul believes it may heal itself only by the destruction of the enemy. At the same time, the death of well-loved comrades induces a grim emulation of their dying:

> Oh, to die this instant, since my friend has had

to fall without getting my help! Very far from his homeland
he has perished, and he did not have me to avert death....
Now I go to find the killer of a man so dear,
Hector; death I shall find at the moment when
Zeus wishes to bring it, he and the other gods.

18.98–100, 114–16

56. The selfsame despair impels toward both death and slaughter:

I know full well that my destiny is to die here,
far from my beloved father and mother; but still
I'll not stop till the Trojans have had a bellyful of war.

19.421–23

57. The man possessed by this double appetite for death belongs, so long as he does not change, to a race quite unlike the race of the living.

58. When the beaten man begs to be allowed to see another day, what response can this meek wish for life find in such hearts? The very possession of arms on one side and their lack on the other divest the imperiled life of nearly all its significance. And, when one has abolished in oneself the thought that to see the light of day is sweet, how will such a one respect that thought in this humble and futile entreaty?

I am at your knees, Achilles; have a thought for me, have mercy;
I am here as a suppliant, O son of Zeus, worthy of respect.
Since at your home I first ate the bread of Demeter,
that day when you seized me in my well-cultivated orchard.
And you sold me, sending me far from my father and my people,
to holy Lemnos; a hecatomb was given for me.
I was ransomed for three times that price; today's dawn is for me
the twelfth since my return to Ilion,
after so many tribulations. I who am now again in your hands
by a baneful destiny. I must be contemptible to Father Zeus,
who again delivers me to you; for a scrap of life only my mother
has borne me, Laothoë, daughter of the aged Altos....

21.74–85

59. What a reply this feeble wish receives!

Come, friend, die also yourself! Why do you complain so?
Patroclus too has died and he was a much better man than you.
And I—do you not see how comely and tall I am?
I am of noble lineage, my mother a goddess;
but for me, too, there is death and a harsh destiny.

There will come a dawn, or an evening, or a midday,
when some warrior with his weapons will strip away my life, too....

21.106–12

60. When one has had to sever oneself from all aspiration for life, it requires a heart-rending effort of altruism to value life in another. One cannot imagine any of Homer's warriors capable of such an effort, except possibly the one who in a sense is at the center of the poem—Patroclus: he "knew how to be gentle to all," and in the *Iliad* he commits no inhumane or cruel act. But how many men have we known of, in many millennia of history, who have evinced such a godlike altruism? One could hardly name two or three. Lacking this altruism, the conquering soldier is like a scourge of nature; possessed by war, he, like a slave, though in an entirely different fashion, becomes a thing, and words have no more appeal to him than to matter. Each, in contact with force, is subjected to its inexorable action, which is to render those it touches either mute or deaf.

61. Such is the character of force. Its power to transform human beings into things is twofold and operates on two fronts; in equal but different ways, it petrifies the souls of those who undergo it and those who ply it. This characteristic reaches its extreme form in the milieu of arms, at the instant when a battle begins to incline toward a decision. Battles are not determined among men who calculate, devise, take resolutions and act on them but among men stripped of these abilities, transformed, fallen to the level either of purely passive inert matter or of the blind forces of sheer impetus. This is the ultimate secret of war, which the *Iliad* expresses in its similes. In these, warriors are likened either to fire, flood, wind, fierce beasts, and whatever blind cause of disaster or to frightened animals, trees, water, sand, whatever is affected by the violence of outside forces. Greeks and Trojans, from day to day, sometimes even from hour to hour, submit by turns to one or the other transformation:

As when a bloodthirsty lion attacks cattle
as they graze in a vast-spreading marshland
by the thousands ...,
... And they all shudder—so then were the Achaeans
in panic put to flight by Hector and Zeus the father,
all of them....

As when destructive fire descends on a thick wood;
and the swirling wind carries it everywhere, then the trunks

uprooted fall under the assault of the violent fire;
just so Agamemnon the son of Atreus made fall the heads of the
fleeing Trojans ....

15.630–32, 636–38; 11.155–59

62. The art of war is merely the art of provoking such metamorphoses, and the tools, the techniques, even the death inflicted on the enemy are only means to this end; it has for its true end the very soul of the combatants. But these metamorphoses pose an enigma, and the gods, who so fascinate us, are their authors. However it happens, this twofold petrifactive property is fundamental to force, and a soul in contact with it eludes it only by a kind of miracle. Such miracles are rare and ephemeral.

63. The thoughtlessness of those that wield force with no regard for men or things they have or believe they have at their mercy, the hopelessness that impels the soldier to devastate, the crushing of the enslaved and the defeated, the massacres, all these things make up a picture of unrelieved horror. Force is its sole hero. A tedious gloom would ensue were there not scattered here and there some moments of illumination—fleeting and sublime moments when men possess a soul. The soul thus roused for an instant, soon to be lost in the empire of force, wakes innocent and unmarred; no ambiguous, complex, or anxious feeling appears in it; courage and love alone have a place there. Sometimes a man discovers his soul during self-deliberation, when he tries, like Hector before Troy, to confront his fate all alone, unaided by gods or men. Other moments when men discover their souls are moments of love; hardly any pure form of love among men is missing from the *Iliad*.

64. The guest-host tradition overcomes the blindness of combat even after several generations have passed:

So I am your beloved guest in the heart of Argos....
Let us avoid each other's spears, even during battle.

6.224–26

65. The love of a son for his parents, and of a father or mother for a son, is always displayed briefly and touchingly:

Thetis answered, shedding tears:
"You were born to me for a brief life, my child, as you say...."

18.94–95

66. So too fraternal love:

My three brothers, whom one mother bore with me,
so beloved....

19.293–94

67. Marital love, doomed to unhappiness, is of a surpassing purity. The spouse, in evoking the disgraces of slavery that await his beloved wife, omits that one the mere thought of which would blot their tenderness. Nothing is so frank as the words his wife addresses to a man about to die:

... It would be better for me,
having lost you, to be under the earth; I will have no
other succor, when you have met your destiny,
only griefs....

6.410–13

68. No less moving are the words spoken to the dead husband:

My husband, dead before your time, so young; and I, your widow,
you have left alone in my house; our child yet small
whom you and I, now unhappy, had together. And I fear
he will never grow up....
For you did not hold my hand and die in bed,
spoke no wise word, that always
I might reflect on night and day shedding tears.

24.725–28, 743–45

69. The most beautiful friendship—that between comrades in arms—forms the theme of the last books of the *Iliad*:

... But Achilles
wept, dreamt of his well-loved comrade; nor did sleep
all-dominating take him; he tossed to and fro ....

24.3–5

70. But the purest triumph of love, the supreme grace of wars, is the friendship that stirs in the hearts of mortal enemies. It can cause to vanish the thirst to avenge a slain son or friend; by an even greater miracle, it can close the gap between benefactor and suppliant, victor and victim:

But when their desire for drink and food was appeased,
then Dardanian Priam started to marvel at Achilles,
how large and handsome he was; he had the look of a god.
And in turn Dardanian Priam was admired by Achilles,
who looked at his handsome face and listened to his words.

And when both were satisfied in contemplating each other ....

24.628–33

71. These moments of grace are infrequent in the *Iliad*, but they suffice to convey with deep regret just what violence has killed and will kill again.

72. However, such an amassing of violent acts would leave one cold but for an accent of incurable bitterness that constantly makes itself felt, even in a single word, turn of a verse, or run-on line. This is what makes the *Iliad* unique, this bitterness emerging from tenderness and enveloping all men equally, like the bright light of the sun. The tone always is imbued with bitterness but never descends to lamentation. Justice and love, totally out of place in this depiction of extremes and unjust violence, subtly and by nuance, drench all with their light. Nothing of value, whether doomed to die or not, is slighted; the misery of all is revealed without dissimulation or condescension; no man is set above or below the common human condition; all that is destroyed is regretted. Victors and victims are equally close to us, and thereby akin to both poet and listener. If there is a discrepancy, it is that the misfortune of enemies is perhaps experienced more grievously.

So he fell there, to sleep the sleep of bronze,
unfortunate man, far from his wife, defending his people ....

11.241–42

73. What a tone to evoke the fate of the youth Achilles sold at Lemnos!

For eleven days he rejoiced in his heart among his loved ones,
after his return from Lemnos; on the twelfth, once more
God delivered him into the hands of Achilles, who had
to send him to Hades, though he did not want to go.

21.45–48

74. And the fate of Euphorbus, who had seen only one day of war:

The blood soaked his hair, hair like that of the Graces....

17.51

75. When Hector is bewailed as

... protector of chaste wives and small children,

24.730

the words suggest purity defiled by force and children offered up to weapons. The spring at the gates of Troy becomes an object of heart-breaking nostalgia when Hector runs past it to save his doomed life:

> There were large basins nearby,
> handsome, all of stone, where the resplendent clothes
> were washed by the women of Troy and their comely daughters,
> in time past, peacetime, before the Achaeans ever came.
> Past these they ran, the one in flight, the other pursuing behind.
>
> 22.153–57

76. The entire *Iliad* is overclouded by the worst of human calamities, the destruction of a city. This calamity could not seem more heartrending if the poet had been born at Troy. But his tone is the same when Achaeans perish far from their homeland.

77. Brief hints of the peacetime world give pain, insofar as this other life, this life of the living, seems tranquil and fulfilling:

> As long as the dawn lasted and the day rose,
> the missiles found their marks on both sides and men fell.
> But at the same hour when the woodcutter goes to prepare his meal
> in the vales of the mountains, when his arms are weary
> from cutting the huge trunks, and his heart has had enough,
> and the hunger for tasty sustenance roils his belly,
> at this hour, the Danaans in their valor broke through the battle-line.
>
> 11.84–90

78. In the *Iliad*, all that exists outside war, all that war destroys or jeopardizes is arrayed in poetry; not so the deeds of war. The transition from life to death is not veiled by any reticence:

> Then his teeth blew out; from both eyes
> the blood started, open-mouthed he spewed blood
> from lips and nostrils; death wrapped him in its black cloud.
>
> 16.348–50

79. The cold brutality of war's deeds is disguised not one iota, since neither victors nor victims are idolized, reviled, or despised. Destiny and the gods almost always determine the shifting fortune of battles. Within the limits imposed by destiny, the gods highhandedly dispense victory and ruin. They are always the ones to provoke the stupidities and betrayals that, time and again, preclude peace; war is their true *métier*, whim and malevolence their only motives. As for the warriors, the similes that liken them—victors and victims—to beasts

or objects can elicit neither admiration nor scorn but only sorrow that men may be so transfigured.

80. The exceptional impartiality that pervades the *Iliad* may have parallels unknown to us, but it has had no imitators. It is difficult to detect that the poet is Greek and not Trojan. The tone of the poem seems to attest directly to the source of its oldest parts; history will perhaps never shed a clear light on this. If one believes with Thucydides that eighty years after the fall of Troy the Achaeans suffered conquest in their turn, one may ask whether these songs, in which iron is seldom mentioned, are not those of the exiled remnants of a conquered people. Constrained to live and die "far from their homeland," like the Greeks fallen at Troy, and having like the Trojans lost their cities, they identified both with the victors, who had been their fathers, and with the victims, whose misery was like their own. The reality of this still-recent war appeared to them across the years, tainted neither by the intoxication of arrogance nor by disgrace. Able to envisage themselves at once as victors or vanquished, they therefore understood what the blinded victors and vanquished could not. This is only a conjecture; one may hardly do more than guess about times so remote.

81. Whatever the case may be, this poem is a miraculous thing. Its bitterness rests on the only just cause for bitterness — the subjection of the human spirit to force, that is, in the last analysis, to inert matter. This subjection is the same for all mortals, though souls bear it differently according to their goodness. No one in the *Iliad* is spared it, just as no one on earth is spared. No one who yields to it is regarded as contemptible for this reason. All who escape the empire of force in their innermost being and in their relations with their fellow men are loved, but loved in grief at the threat of constantly impending destruction. Such is the spirit of the only true epic that the West possesses. The *Odyssey* seems only a good reproduction of the *Iliad* in some places, of oriental poems in others. The *Aeneid* is an imitation, granted a brilliant one, marred by frigidity, ostentation, and poor taste. The *chansons de geste*, lacking impartiality, fall short of grandeur; the author and the reader of the *Chanson de Roland* do not feel the death of an enemy as they do that of Roland.

82. Attic tragedy, at any rate that of Aeschylus and Sophocles, is the true descendant of epic. The concept of justice enlightens it without ever interfering in it. Force here appears in its cold rigidity,

always attended by the lethal effects that neither those who use it nor those who suffer it may escape. The abasement of the soul under its coercion is neither disguised, nor mitigated by facile pity, nor held up to scorn. More than one being wounded by the degradation of misfortune is offered for us to wonder at. The Gospels are the final splendid expression of the Greek genius, as the *Iliad* is the first. The spirit of Greece may be seen here not only in the command to seek "the kingdom and the justice of our heavenly Father" to the exclusion of every other goal but also in the revelation of human misery in a being at once divine and human. The accounts of the Passion show that a divine spirit, joined with flesh, is affected by unhappiness. It shudders before suffering and death and feels itself in the depths of anguish isolated from men and from God. The experience of human misery gives these accounts that nuance of simplicity that typifies the Greek genius and so charges Attic tragedy and the *Iliad* with value. Certain words strike a note curiously similar to that of the epic: the Trojan youth, sent unwilling to Hades, comes to mind when Christ says to Peter: "Another will gird you and carry you where you do not want to go." This nuance is intrinsic to the spirit of the Gospels, since the experience of human misery is a requirement of justice and love. Whoever fails to grasp that every human soul is subject to changing fortune and necessity can neither regard as peers nor love as himself those separated from him by the chasm of chance. The diverse restrictions that weigh on men give birth to the illusion of discrete species incapable of communicating. It is impossible to love and to be just unless one understands the realm of force and knows enough not to respect it.

83. The links between the human soul and destiny, to what extent each soul selects its own ideal, what pitiless necessity modifies in the soul according to the vagaries of fortune, what elements virtue and grace can preserve intact—in such questions lies are seductively easy. Arrogance, degradation, hatred, contempt, insensibility, the wish to forget or overlook—all contribute to this temptation. In particular, nothing is more rare than a just presentation of misfortune. In depicting it, one nearly always pretends that abasement is innate in the unfortunate or that the soul may endure misfortune unscathed, without its thoughts being uniquely altered. The Greeks had a force of soul that allowed them, for the most part, to avoid self-delusion; they were compensated for this by understanding how to attain in all

things the highest degree of insight, purity, and simplicity. But the spirit transmitted from the *Iliad* to the Gospels via the philosophers and tragic poets hardly ever breached the borders of Greek civilization; and, after the fall of Greece, nothing remained but reflections of that spirit.

84. The Romans and Hebrews both thought themselves exempt from common human misfortune, the former as a nation destined to be master of the world, the latter by the favor of their God and precisely in proportion as they were obedient to him. The Romans despised foreigners, enemies, the vanquished, their subjects, their slaves; thus they had neither epics nor tragedies. They substituted gladiators for tragedies. The Hebrews saw misfortune as indicative of sin and consequently a proper justification for contempt. They considered their beaten foes repellent to God himself and damned to atone for crimes; this made cruelty permissible, even mandatory. Thus no passage of the Old Testament strikes a chord comparable to that of Greek epic, except possibly certain parts of the Book of Job. Throughout twenty centuries of Christianity, Romans and Hebrews have been admired, read, emulated in deeds and words, cited whenever a crime needed justification.

85. Moreover, the spirit of the Gospels was not handed down uncontaminated through successive generations of Christians. From the beginning, the joyful willingness of martyrs to suffer and die was deemed a sign of grace, as if grace could do more for men than for Christ. Those who consider that even God himself, once he had become human, contemplated the severity of destiny with a tremor of anguish ought to know that human misery may be disregarded only by those who have camouflaged the severity of destiny in their own eyes by an illusion, an intoxication, or a figment of the imagination. The man unshielded by an armor of lies cannot suffer force without its defiling his very soul. Grace may forestall this taint from corrupting, but it cannot prevent the wound. Having forgotten it so thoroughly, the Christian tradition has only very seldom recovered the simplicity that makes each phrase of the Passion narratives so poignant. On the other hand, the practice of forcible conversion concealed the effects of force on the souls of those wielding it.

86. Notwithstanding the brief intoxication with rediscovered Greek literature during the Renaissance, the Greek genius has not revived in twenty centuries. Something of it appears in Villon,

Shakespeare, Cervantes, Molière, and once in Racine. Human misery, vis-à-vis love, is stripped bare in *L'École des Femmes* and in *Phèdre*; an odd century to be sure, which, contrary to the epic era, perceived the misery of man only in love, while always cloaking in glory the results of force in warfare and in politics. One might possibly cite a few other names, but nothing the peoples of Europe have produced matches their first known poem. They will perhaps rediscover epic genius when they learn to believe nothing is protected from fate, learn never to admire force, not to hate the enemy nor to scorn the unfortunate. It is doubtful whether this will soon occur.

PART IV

Commentary

Paragraphs 1–6

Simone Weil states her thesis immediately and bluntly. Force is the actual subject of the first work of European literature, specifically its deleterious effects on human beings. The most obvious of these effects is to metamorphose the living into the dead, to turn what it touches into inert matter, a thing. This is no mere transition to another state of life, as, for instance, those who believe in an "afterlife" of heavenly bliss may expect. Homer's characters have no hopes of a personal immortality to compensate adequately for the loss of this life. The *Iliad* is a poem of war; peacetime activities pictured in the epic serve only to heighten the sense of war's brutality.

1. Weil's opening statement throws down a gauntlet: Homer's poem is not what it has appeared to be to generations of its readers. The *Iliad* is not so much about the Trojan war and the military adventures of Greeks and Trojans as it is about force, understood not simply as a physical phenomenon, the result of an equation (mass times acceleration, or the like), but as an active entity, capable of profound, always negative, influences on the lives it touches. Furthermore, the picture painted in the *Iliad* holds true for our own times as well, any comforting but illusory notions of civilization's progress notwithstanding.

2. Weil now directly defines "force" as that which makes people over into things, that is, corpses. And it accomplishes this in an instant. The passage quoted from Book 11 describes a moment in Agamemnon's *aristeia* (period when a single individual is preeminent in battle). Trojan charioteers cut down by the Greek hero are

no longer young men attractive to their wives—they are carrion. This image of spouses or families destroyed by force is especially poignant for Weil and recurs throughout the essay. Here the shattered families are anonymous. The next paragraphs focus on a particular hero and his wife.

3. The dragged warrior in the passage from Book 22 is Hector, son of King Priam and greatest of the Trojan champions. His handsome body, now a lifeless thing, is savagely mutilated by the victorious Achilles. Homer's focus on the detail of the fallen hero's hair adds to the pathos of the scene. The adjective used to denote the hair's darkness, *kuaneai* (κυάνεαι), is most often used of the gods; see Richardson (1993) 148: "with characteristic economy, the poet draws our attention to the contrast between Hektor's 'god-like' appearance and his defilement"; and Griffin (1980) 138: "Homeric pathos can go no further than this.... The bitterness of the ill-treatment of Hector's head ... is increased by his enemy having the power to inflict it in his own fatherland, before the eyes of his own people." So, too, Vergil highlights the blood-caked beard and hair of Hector in Aeneas's nightmare at *Aeneid* 2.277–79.

4. There is nothing to soften the ugliness of the image. Hector will go to no heavenly reward, no better lot in the next world. (Homer's Hades is not a consoling prospect: see, e.g., Achilles' words at *Od.* 11.488–91.) His soul departs indignant at the premature loss of young manhood. Weil overlooks here the Homeric hero's investment in the ethos of glory: to have participated in the "noble deeds of men," *klea andron* (κλέα ἀνδρῶν), deeds that will live on in human memory, is thought to be sufficient compensation for the loss of one's life (cf. Hector to his wife Andromache at 6.440–49 or Sarpedon to Glaucus at 12.315–28). For discussion of this lacuna in Weil's interpretation, see Ferber (1981) 72–74.

5. Compare this undiluted ferocity with the normal routine of daily life in Hector's home, as Andromache and her handmaidens prepare for the expected arrival of the beloved husband and master as if he were returning as usual from his "day at the office." Richardson (1993) 155 notes that the phrase "on his return from combat" (μάχης ἐκ νοστήσαντι) "is always used of warriors who are fated *not* to survive" and Postlethwaite (2000) 277 that lines 443–44 contain "the irony that it will be as a corpse that Hektor

will be bathed, and that Andromache will be denied even this consolation by Achilleus' continued abuse of the body."

6. Such creature comforts as warm baths are rare in the *Iliad* and, as Weil points out in widening the perspective of her reflections, rare in life in general.

Paragraphs 7–13

Weil turns now from the most obvious and coarse operation of force to others that are more subtle, more insidious, and ultimately more horrific, because they bring about the paradox of a "living death." Turning to the first category of the living dead, she discusses the experience of the defeated enemy reduced to supplicating his conqueror in order to remain alive. Such an individual is "alive" only vegetatively; he is, in the eyes of those around him, already a thing and no longer a present living entity worthy of attention. One thinks of Ralph Ellison's title, *The Invisible Man*, chosen to suggest the condition of those who are ignored or "unseen" as living souls by virtue of what Weil would have called the "force" of racial prejudice. (The oppression of blacks was a subject that interested her: see Pétrement [1976] 478.) On supplication in Homer generally, see Gould (1973), Pedrick (1982), and Crotty (1994): "Supplication ... has a moral dimension, for it provides the one supplicated with an occasion for insight into the contours of mortal life—its vulnerability to circumstance, and the seriousness of the claim another's suffering has to one's attention" (xi).

7. Weil describes abstractly the paralysis force imposes not only in killing but in the very prospect of killing. Persons at the mercy of a superior force mimic the dead. They are queer entities, part vital (possessing a soul), part inert. The conjunction of soul and thing is a perversion of the natural order, a sad deformity common in such an environment.

8. Now a specific illustration: Lycaon, a son of Priam, beaten and assuming the posture of the suppliant before the victorious Achilles. Once before, Lycaon had fallen into Achilles' hands. On that occasion, Achilles had been content to sell his Trojan captive into slavery, from which he was subsequently ransomed by his family (21.76–80). This time, however, the death of Patroclus has made

Achilles deaf to any negotiated release of enemy captives: "You fool, don't mention ransom to me, nor propose it" (21.99).

9. Lycaon recognizes that he is already mere matter. He cannot evade the sword that concentrates force to a lethal hardness and sharpness; the death blow only completes an inexorable process. Paralyzed in life, he awaits the final paralysis of death. Cf. Richardson (1993) 63: "Lukaon lets go of Akhilleus' spear and knees before he is struck.... Lukaon's gesture [stretching forth his hands] ... indicates his despair."

10. The paralysis of the suppliant is so complete that he lacks even the galvanic response, as normally involuntary reactions are suspended in the proximity of deadly force. In the passage quoted from Book 24, the proud king, Priam, abjectly kisses the hands stained with the blood of his own son.

11. In a strange inversion of affect during a scene that breaks many patterns of behavior in the *Iliad*, Achilles the killer shudders at the sight of Priam, in the way people shudder at the sight of a known murderer. Weil's comment on 24.480–84 is a rare case of misunderstanding or misrepresentation. Priam is not in quite the same position as other suppliants in the *Iliad*, already dead before actual death; that is, he is not "un cadavre." In Homer's words, which Weil faithfully renders, Priam causes a shudder in the beholder as would a murderer ("Il a tué"), not a corpse. Cf. Postlethwaite (2000) 302: "The simile asserts the authority of Achilleus, by comparing him to the man of substance with power of life and death, and it points up the status of Priam as suppliant by making him an exile in his own land"; also Heiden (1998) 2 on "an emotional intensification achieved through the particular contrasts presented by this simile ...," and Knox (1990) 59 [idem (1994) 39–40]: "For Achilles, a child of the quarrelsome, violent society of the Achaeans ..., the appearance of a distinguished stranger and his gesture of supplication evoke the familiar context of the man of violence seeking shelter. Achilles cannot imagine the truth."

12. The suppliant, at the mercy of superior force, does not long command attention, because he has already started to approximate a thing. Achilles' thoughts turn to his own father, Peleus, and to his dead friend, Patroclus, just as if Priam were not present at all. Weil's analysis here and in the next paragraph depends on a misleading translation in line 508: *un peu* ("a little") does not convey

the Greek ἦκα, which means "gently." Achilles pushes the old man gently, being distracted by anguish rather than uninhibited because he discounts Priam's humanity. He may also be indicating nonverbally his discomfiture at Priam's plea; see Lateiner (1995) 51: "Akhilleus acknowledges the enemy's suppliancy but gently distances Priam from himself by force.... Distance talks; he has expressed proxemic need for 'personal space' and reduced for himself the 'volume' or intensity of Priam's unanswerable plea." Cf. Postlethwaite (2000) 303: "Achilleus' action ... breaks the bond of physical intimacy Priam established by kissing his hands, and replaces it with a bond of emotional intimacy which allows them both to indulge their grief openly.... Achilleus' gentleness towards Priam contrasts with Agamemnon's roughness towards Chryses (1.25)."

13. Weil elaborates on the peculiar lack of "presence" of the suppliant. We do not normally behave the same in the presence of others as when we are alone. Achilles in Book 24 shows by a certain casualness in his gestures — for example, pushing old Priam away — that he does not feel the normal influence a living person has on those in his presence. Weil maintains that the Trojan king is already a thing in Achilles' eyes, and indeed in his own, since he shows no indignation at such treatment. He has begun to "imitate nonentity." Cf. Macleod (1982) 130: "Priam's posture at this point [24.510] is as humiliating as can be." He fears to express a desire lest he provoke the force that, as Achilles pointedly informs him (24.568–70), can easily destroy him. Priam can only tremble and obey.

Paragraphs 14–23

A second category of death-in-life is slavery. While the suppliant may hope, however forlornly, to escape the realm of force if his plea is heeded, the slave has become a thing for the rest of his life. Such a person is a kind of zombie: part living being, part corpse. Weil's first example is Chryseis, whose enslavement is the root cause of the quarrel between Agamemnon and Achilles that motivates the action of the *Iliad*. Others destined to slavery, if they survive the war, are Andromache and her infant son Astyanax. Again, as in describing the death of Hector, Weil seizes on the disruption and disintegration of family happiness as an especially moving consequence of the operation of force.

In the *Iliad*, slavery is a fate worse than death; Hector wishes to be dead rather than live to witness the enslavement of his wife and son. And, for slaves themselves, the psychological effects are dreadful. Priam the suppliant bows and obeys for a short while and with a specific objective. Slaves bow and obey throughout lives benumbed and benighted by the absence of any goal. They may not even indulge in an emotion unapproved by their master. True feelings must be suppressed or expressed only under the guise of sympathy with the master. Force cancels all genuine inner life in slaves. It is as relentless as nature itself. One can no more elude its influence than one can elude hunger.

14. The state of death-in-life that Weil identified in the case of a suppliant is not the worst effect of force on human beings, since it persists only for moments before death or deliverance. For other unfortunates, such as slaves, death-in-life is a permanent status. The slave is an object for the remainder of his life, his lacerated soul trapped in a body that is held as a material possession.

15. Weil's first example of this "hybrid of man and corpse" is Chryseis, the young daughter of the priest Chryses. The *Iliad* begins with the old priest's supplication of the Achaeans (1.15) for the return of his beloved daughter, who, like Achilles' prize, Briseis, has been taken captive during fighting and pillaging around the Troad. Agamemnon refuses him, thereby, as Latacz et al. (2000) 37 points out, overruling without further discussion the will of all the assembled Achaeans, who "cried out in favour/ that the priest be respected" (1.22–23, trans. Lattimore [1951]). This prompts Chryses to appeal to Apollo, who duly afflicts the Achaean army with a plague. In the passage quoted, Agamemnon cruelly taunts the old priest with the vision of his daughter growing old in slavery far from home, serving her master menially and sexually. Though heartless, this forecast simply reflected the customary fate of women captured in war. See Kirk (1985) 56: "The sentence is a powerful one typical of Agamemnon at his nastiest" and Pulleyn (2000) 131: "It is undeniably brutal for him to taunt Chryses with the prospect of his sexual enjoyment of his daughter but he re-

peatedly shows the same traits in Book 1 and elsewhere. At 6.58–60 he expresses the wish that no Trojan will escape doom, not even the unborn male babies in their mothers' wombs—a repellent image."

16. The second example is Andromache as Hector imagines her fate during their interview in Book 6. Though Hector will not live to see the day of his wife's enslavement, he suffers in advance as he foresees her lot. The word "necessity," *ananke* (ἀνάγκη), in line 458 had specially strong resonances for Weil; she quoted the line in Greek as the epigraph to her "Factory Journal" in Weil (1951) 45. In this Iliadic context, *ananke* denotes the harsh, unavoidable reality of the slave's plight.

17. After Hector's death, Andromache knows that she and her son, Astyanax, will soon suffer enslavement. What Hector had pictured in his imagination in Book 6 is frightfully imminent in Book 24. Cf. Richardson (1993) 354: "whether [Astyanax] is actually present or not we are not told, but the pathos of the apostrophe is the same."

18. It would be better to die: Hector has had the easy way out. For slavery reduces an individual to a shell, bereft of anger or dreams, and nearly even of the memories that constitute a personality. Slaves are forever deprived of their homes and their own.

19. Slaves may exhibit emotion or grieve only in empathy with their masters. The slaves' pent-up anguish at their own plight and that of their loved ones may express itself only disguisedly: for example, Briseis and the other captive women who lament the dead Patroclus in Book 19 are alleviating their own personal heartaches. Griffin (1980) 68 distinguishes Briseis's genuine grief for gentle Patroclus from that of the other enslaved women, who weep for their own personal fates, but Shay (1994) 134 rightly observes that "even [Briseis's] grief for [her husband and brothers] is shown in a demeaning fashion.... Because Achilles was stronger and killed Briseis's husband, she'll like him better anyway. The overall effect is pornographic, a male fantasy that a woman *wants* to be raped by any man strong enough to kill her husband and carry her away."

20. Like a draft animal whose physical energy is channeled in one direction only, the emotional energy, the love, within the slave may take only the master as its object. Thus we confront the grim

paradox of the slave required to divert her love and devotion from her husband and brothers to the man who slaughtered them. Briseis, as she grieves Patroclus, may seem to have precious little to thank him for, but in consoling her with the thought of marriage to Achilles, he was in truth bestowing the only kindness available to a slave. But that promised relationship will also end in grief: "That Briseis had been married adds to the pathos of her mourning a second time over a man ...; a third repetition of her sorrow will soon come when Akhilleus himself dies" — Edwards (1991) 270.

21. Weil now makes a rather peculiar analogy, one motivated, I believe, by her own personal experience (she was anorexic throughout her adult life). She notes again the annihilation of inner life that force brings about and then compares the inevitability of that annihilation to the operation of nature. Specifically, she reminds us of the story of Niobe as Achilles recounts it in Book 24. Achilles, who had himself once refused to eat because of the intensity of his grief for Patroclus (19.199–214), is here encouraging Priam to break the paralysis of sorrow long enough to take a meal. He convinces the old man by appealing to the precedent of Niobe, who had lost twelve children, and lost them through her own fault. She grieved them inconsolably for nine days as they lay unburied (Hector, too, has been kept unburied for nine days). But then she remembered to eat, says Homer, embellishing the myth to suit Achilles' persuasive purposes; see Kakridis (1949) 96–105 and Edwards (1987) 67: "The fact that Niobe ate, even while grieving, was invented by the poet to fit the myth to the situation." Despite Niobe's love for her children and her psychic turmoil, she could evade nature's appetitive processes no more than she could defeat death to save their lives. As Weil herself stated the moral: "It is not true that human love is stronger than death. Death is much stronger. Love is subdued to death" — Weil (1970) 323. On further similarities between Priam and Niobe, see Macleod (1982) 139–40 and Edwards (1987) 311.

22. Just as men and women in general must live within certain limitations imposed by nature on the human will, so too, the slave must live within the far more severe limitations imposed by force on man's inner life. For Simone Weil, who strove so hard all her life to restrain the natural desire for food, the example of the triumph

of nature over the mind in the case of Niobe was especially mean-ingful: "Those moments when one is compelled to look on mere existence as the sole end represent total, unmixed horror. Therein lies the horror of the situation of the man condemned to death, and which Christ himself experienced. 'Niobe also, of the beauti-ful hair, thought of eating.' That is sublime, in the same way as space in the frescoes of Giotto. A humiliation which forces one to renounce even despair" — Weil (1956b) 546. Cf. Kakridis (1949) 97: "Who has not experienced in his own life-time this hard struggle between the soul, immersed in grief, and the flesh with its necessi-ties ever more imperiously demanding satisfaction—till those necessities finally conquer."

23. Just as the pangs of hunger are beyond human control, so, too, the victim of force is subjected to unrelievable disgrace and sorrow. Moreover, Zeus simply visits these trials on the unfortunate. Weil, in a letter to a young poet she had met during Easter services at Solesmes in 1938, linked the passage cited here with the suffering of Christ: "It was not till Christ had known the physical agony of crucifixion, the shame of blows and mockery, that he uttered his immortal cry, a question which shall remain unanswered through all times on this earth 'My God, why hast thou forsaken me?' [Matt. 27:46 = Mark 15:34]. When poetry struggles toward the ex-pressing of pain and misery, it can be great poetry only if that cry sounds through every word. So it does in the *Iliad* [24.531–33]" — Weil (1965) 103. Homer's warriors are—all of them, ultimately— forsaken by their father, Zeus. Achilles' story of Zeus's two urns "is consolatory and foreshadows the themes of later *consolationes*, which express sympathy but correct the tendency to excessive grief, by pointing out that weeping has no physical use, suffering is common to us all..." — Richardson (1993) 329; cf. Sheppard (1922) 203: "It is no irrelevant parable, but the central doctrine which gives nobility to Homer's vision of our tragic life."

Paragraphs 24–32

Weil now observes that the world of the *Iliad* is not divided simplisti-cally between wretched victims and triumphant conquerors. Given time, force afflicts all without exception. For example, warriors are compelled to accept mistreatment from their superiors. Homer's poem contains examples of both low-status and high-status individuals suffering abuse. Even Achilles is humbled by Agamemnon, who is humbled in turn.

On the battlefield, too, there is no such thing as uninterrupted success. The mass of warriors on one side may be cowed at one moment by their opponents' champion, but in the next moment their own champion reverses the balance of self-confidence. Even the seemingly invincible Achilles is intimidated in battle, albeit by an elemental opponent. Again, it is not the intrinsic worth or superior effort of combatants that determines the outcome; it is rather blind destiny, supervised by the amoral Greek gods.

24. Turning from the obvious and hapless victims of force, Weil asserts that the apparent possessors of superior force also succumb in their turn. Any man may, at any time, be beaten down. Even undefeated warriors have to yield, as when Odysseus in Book 2 prevents the men of the rank and file from taking flight by assaulting them physically and verbally. Cf. Kirk (1985) 136–37: "the use of the royal sceptre … as an instrument for pushing the troops around is a little surprising, although understandable in the circumstances.... Heroic rebuke tends to be exaggerated, even unfair.... The troops have, in fact, simply been obeying their commander...."

25. Thersites is a specific example of this. This agitator criticizes his commanders in terms strongly reminiscent of Achilles' rebuke to Agamemnon and his fellow soldiers in Book 1; see Postlethwaite (2000) 52–53 and idem (1988). Odysseus silences him not with a rational counter-argument but simply with an exhibition of superior strength to the applause of onlookers who do not appreciate their own vulnerability to such arbitrary mistreatment. It should be noted that the "irritation" (French *peine*) felt by the witnesses to Thersites' comeuppance is "because of all the recent confusion as well as the bad taste left by Thersites' harangue ..., not because of his present sufferings, which they find amusing"—Kirk (1985) 144.

26. This subjection to force is not the lot of common soldiers only. We see even the mighty Achilles frustrated by his commander-in-chief. In Book 1, he sits apart from his fellow warriors weeping in

self-pity and exasperation. As Latacz (2000) 126 comments, the aggrieved Achilles' withdrawal to the seashore and petition to a divinity parallel the actions of the aggrieved Chryses earlier and portend equally deadly consequences for the Greek army.

27. Agamemnon gloats that he has shown Achilles his place and that no one will try again to question his preeminence. The operative word in line 186 is *pherteros* (φέρτερος), meaning "superior"; cf. Kirk (1985) 72: "there is an implied contrast with κρατερός ["strong," "mighty"] in 178. Akhilleus may be stronger in battle, but Agamemnon is his superior overall, and that is what counts"; Zanker (1994) 76: "Agamemnon in his conflict with Achilles feels a need to humiliate Achilles to put him in his place.... Such humiliation is only called for when a real threat is involved."

28. But within a few days, in Book 9, Agamemnon will bitterly regret his actions and, weeping in his turn (9.13–15), humble himself by sending a formal embassy to petition the offended Achilles and offer him rich compensation—all to no avail. Cf. Willcock (1976) 95: "He is overcome ... by the loss of prestige which he is suffering in the defeat of the Greeks."

29. No warrior escapes dishonor. In Book 7, the whole Greek army— Achilles and his men excepted—is overawed by the mighty Hector, when he issues his invitation to single combat.

30. Moments later, Ajax strikes fear into the hearts of the Trojans, including Hector himself: "The vision of Aias taking huge strides forward, wielding his great spear and smiling dangerously, is unforgettable and produces immediate effects on those present ..." —Kirk (1990) 262.

31. Ajax's success is not unbroken, however, and he must retreat during the great battle a few days later, in Books 11–18. He is dehumanized by fear, "like a beast."

32. Even Achilles tastes fear when, in the midst of his *aristeia*, he is confronted by the indignant river god Scamander in Book 21.211–327 (see esp. lines 246–48). No amount of courage or physical strength or will power can ensure permanent success for a warrior. Destiny apportions suffering to all at the appointed time, regardless of the qualities of poor mortals. As we see in the scene of Zeus's scales in Book 8, it is all quite outside any rational control, even by the gods themselves. Zeus only holds the scales; he does not decide which pan will rise, which fall. Cf. Wilson (1996)

182: "There is no suggestion at all that the weighing of the scales in itself represents any partisanship on Zeus' part ..."; so too, Willcock (1976) 86–87, *pace* Postlethwaite (2000) 122–23: "the metaphor of Zeus' golden scales is a dramatic representation of his own decision...."

Paragraphs 33–46

Weil now turns to a discussion of the blind impartiality of destiny: all men who agree to the exercise of force by their participation in war are doomed to suffer. Those who live by the sword die by it. But those who would live in peace are also destined to suffer. In human life, neither strength nor weakness is a permanent condition. The problem is that no one seems capable of recognizing this crucial fact. Weak and strong think they are utterly disparate species. The strong feel no brake on their momentum; they do as they will with no pause to consider that what they inflict on others might one day be inflicted on themselves. There is no forethought. "Do unto others as you would have them do unto you" has no place in such a world.

The possession of force always spawns delusions of grandeur. It is inconceivable to the strong that their power may be limited. Thus they exceed the bounds of the force temporarily at their disposal and enter the province of chance, where nothing may shield them. By their transgression of limits, they invite the swift and mathematically certain penalty the Greeks knew as "Nemesis" (righteous punishment or retribution personified). Unlike the Greeks, we in the West have lost the notion of Nemesis, of an omniscient agency that punishes the abuse of force. We have no sense of balance in affairs of force. Homer's poem teaches us about such balance. For it is an account of shifting fortune, of the seesaw motion of victory and defeat. But this game of seesaw is imperceptible to its participants. In the course of the poem, the Greeks have a chance to achieve their ostensible war aims but let it pass in hopes of "total" victory. On the other side, Hector, even knowing the consequences of defeat for his loved ones, is willing to risk all to achieve "total" victory over the Greeks. Each side suffers from decisions shaped by the intoxication with excess. Even Achilles, who appears to have the ultimate victory in our epic, is destined to die soon after Hector. When force is involved, there are no true victors, only victims.

33. Weil contends that destiny, which dispenses suffering impartially in the *Iliad*, approximates the notion of blind justice. The aphoristic "Ares is just and kills those who kill" anticipates for her such biblical passages as Matt. 26:52: "All who take the sword die by the sword" (cf. Gen. 9:6: "Anyone who sheds human blood, for that human being his blood will be shed"). Cf. Weil (1956b) 40: "To kill is always to kill oneself." In 18.309, Ares is not named; rather he is designated by his epithet Enyalios (Ἐνυάλιος). Edwards (1991) 182 notes that the phrase ξυνὸς Ἐνυάλιος, literally, "Enyalios [is] shared [by all]," quickly achieved proverbial status in Greek literature.

34. Weil returns to the themes of delusion and impermanence in the empire of force. The strong and the weak feel they are not one species and that their situations are everlasting. Achilles says exactly this to Hector at 22.262–67: lions and men, wolves and sheep may have no mutual understandings. Cf. Gottschall (2001) 286: "In his similes, [Homer] ubiquitously imagines Greeks and Trojans as members of different species. The attacking warrior, most often Greek, is envisioned as a predator ... and the defender is envisioned as a member of a prey species.... Achilles provides a veritable definition and illustration of cultural pseudospeciation in his beautiful and cruel 'between lions and men' speech." Those who "possess" force move mindlessly, without even an instant of deliberation in which to evaluate right and wrong or to take any thought for the future. They vaunt over the defeated enemy (cf. Patroclus taunting the dying "acrobat" Cebriones in 16.733–53); Achilles engages in human sacrifice (23.175–76). Priestly old men are insulted but so too are warriors in their prime. The nullifying of all reasonable appreciation of consequences leads the heroes straight to death.

35. The world of the *Iliad* is one of unrecognized human limits, of boundaries transgressed by the victim-possessors of force. The heroes repeatedly go beyond their limits and expose themselves to the operation of chance. Weil may be influenced here by Thucydides' observations about the role of chance, *tukhe* (τύχη), in war: "Consider ... the large role of the unpredictable in war.... The

longer the war goes on, the more matters hinge on accidents....
When people embark on war, they do things backwards. First
they act, and only when they have already suffered do they begin
to think" (Thuc. 1.78.1–3; cf. 3.45.6–7). Weil was reading inten-
sively in the ancient historians in the years immediately before the
outbreak of World War II — see Pétrement (1976) 345.

36. Weil, whose brother André became an eminent mathematician,
was interested in Pythagorean philosophy and the role of number
and proportion in Greek thought. For her, there was a kind of
mathematical precision about the Greek notion of Nemesis.
Transgression necessarily entails redress: such is the all-pervasive
message of Greek tragedy and philosophy. Weil suggests that the
Greek concept may be detected too in the Buddhist idea of karma.
She conjectures that there may have been cultural contact between
Greece and India via Phoenicia and Lycia even as early as the second millennium B.C.; here she was influenced by Charles Autran's
theories on the subject (1938–39–44), to which she alludes in a letter to her brother in 1940: "the theory [that Lycians and Phoeni-
cians were Dravidians] is very attractive — too attractive, even — in
this sense, that it offers an extremely simple explanation of the
analogies between Greek thought and Indian thought" — Weil
(1965) 118–19. For Weil, the sad fact is that we in the West have
lost this sense of proportion and balance: to be sure, we measure
quantifiable, material things, but we have not continued the Greek
practice of measure in the realm of morality.

37. To illustrate the lack of reasonable calculation in those whom
force has intoxicated, Weil cites instances of warriors foolishly
forgoing the opportunity to get what, supposedly, they have gone
to war for. Warriors in a position of superiority forget the inescapable and rapid fluctuations of warfare. After Ajax gets the
better of Hector in the duel in Book 7, Diomedes, in his typically
over-confident manner (cf. 9.32–49), urges his approving fellow
warriors not to be content with achievement of the stated goals of
the campaign — booty and Helen — but to yearn instead for abso-
lute victory. Cf. Zanker (1994) 48: "Diomedes appears to have
forgotten the real reason for the Achaians' expedition, which has
become submerged in his mind by a desire to press on to nothing
less than the total destruction of Troy." Mueller (1984) 67 goes so
far as to claim that Homer "holds that war does not come into its

own until its 'original' cause is lost." The non-Homeric tale that Helen was actually in Egypt during the war is to be found in Herodotus 2.112–20; variations on the same theme go back at least to the sixth-century epico-lyric poet Stesichorus and culminate in Euripides' *Helen*. Cf. Austin (1994).

38. The Greeks unwisely commit themselves to total war; they want to kill all their enemies, enslave all the women and children, seize all the spoils. They forget that none of this is within their power— yet. Many, including ultimately Achilles himself, will perish before such a goal is reached. Much is still up to chance.

39. Hector, during his conversation with Andromache in Book 6, seems to know full well the fate awaiting him and his city (as does Priam: "Andromakhe's fate is paralleled at 22.62 and 65, where Priam foresees his daughters and sisters-in-law being dragged along ... if Hektor is killed and Troy falls"—Kirk [1990] 223). See Schadewaldt (1997a) 135: "Before Hector too stands the destiny of his death. But ... this fate expands immediately into the common fate of his people.... Behind this knowledge of the future destruction lies an unspoken 'But all the same!' To fight, Hector does not need even hope."

40. Two days later (French *surlendemain*; it is actually the third day later), after a taste of battlefield success, Hector is unwilling to let the Greeks depart for fear of losing the chance to make them "carry wound marks ... to digest at home." He wants to make an example of them to forestall similar attacks in the future. Schadewaldt (1997b) 161: "[Hector's] *persona* passes into a sinister twilight ..."; cf. Schein (1984) 182: "He knows, of course, that [his own death] will come at some time and that it is unavoidable ..., but in contrast to Achilles, who seems more than human because he can accept how human he is, Hektor is merely human, and cannot—will not—accept this knowledge." Redfield (1975) 123 prefers to see in the interview between Hector and Andromache the warrior's commitment to a larger altruism: "The warrior when he goes to war immerses himself in the collectivity. There is thus a tension between obligations to household and to city, for in defending everyone the warrior must set aside his special obligations to those who are most truly his own."

41. Hector succeeds in keeping the Greeks pinned down, but chance turns the tide in favor of Agamemnon, whose *aristeia* in Book 11 reduces the Trojans to fleeing cattle.
42. In the course of the great day of battle recounted in Books 11–18, Hector retreats, then regains the advantage, even pushing the Greeks back to the sea, then is repulsed by Patroclus, then kills Patroclus. When it is clear to cooler heads that Achilles is now likely to re-enter the fray and to exact a terrible price for the death of his friend, Hector quashes the advice given him by the infuriatingly prudent sage Polydamas (18.254–283). Force has blinded him to the realities of war and has even made him forget the awesome prowess of Achilles.
43. Hector has painted himself into a corner, for the next day, as he stands to face the onslaught of Achilles, his options are limited by the foolish and costly bravado of his earlier words to Polydamas. Cf. Richardson (1993) 117: "In the eyes of those who look on, Hektor initially displays a stubborn determination to stand firm. But the poet reveals to us that internally he is in a turmoil of uncertainty ..."; and Zanker (1994) 61: "he has the added shame of knowing that his self-confidence has proven inadequate and that a lesser warrior is in a position to rebuke him for it."
44. Hector pays the full price for his folly and lack of foresight in the moment of victory. As the seesaw of war shifts, he loses the advantage of force and runs a race of shame for his very life.
45. He becomes a suppliant, that hapless and miserable "living thing," here begging that Achilles will allow his corpse to be ransomed and not feed it to the dogs. "This speech is the final one in a series of pleas by Trojans for their lives, all vain ..."—Richardson (1993) 141.
46. But even as Achilles wins his greatest triumph at the climax of the *Iliad*, his victory is overshadowed by the certain knowledge, conveyed by the gods themselves—Thetis repeatedly but also Hera via equine ventriloquism (19.404–17)—that his life is forfeit and that he too will suffer death on the battlefield. Ares kills those who kill. No exceptions.

Paragraphs 47–60

Weil restates her principal thesis: force disfigures all whom it touches, wielder and victim alike. In this light, all human beings are innocent, because all are in fact victims. Achilles sees the truth of this in a reflective mood in Book 24. Force effectively shuts out such reflection because it infects souls with immoderation. To speak of moderation in force would be like speaking of heat in ice or evenness in odd. True, some individuals (Thersites, Achilles, Polydamas) occasionally speak for reason, but their words are unheeded. In the world of the *Iliad*, the gods intervene if necessary to thwart reason. Failing any sane explanation, the men ascribe to higher powers the horrors of life under force. Their outlook is deeply fatalistic. Weil (1973b) 138: "None of them knows why each sacrifices himself and all his family to a bloody and aimless war, and that is why, all through the poem, it is the gods who are credited with the mysterious influence which nullifies peace negotiations, continually revives hostilities, and brings together again the contending forces urged by a flash of good sense to abandon the struggle."

The resignation of warriors is acquired only through experience. They set out to war in a celebratory mood, blithely unaware of the harsh necessities about to be imposed upon them. And for a time during the early stages of war, the mood of play can be sustained. But fear, defeat, and the death of comrades soon bludgeon all comforting illusions out of the souls of warriors, souls soon further debilitated by the stark prospect of their own death. This prospect, faced every single day, replaces all other concepts of the future; death is the only imaginable outcome. This is the most bitter fatalism. The soul cannot conceive of any release from force except—ironically—by the further exercise of force. Erich Maria Remarque vividly portrayed this spiritual malaise in *All Quiet on the Western Front*: "I often sit over against myself, as before a stranger, and wonder how the unnameable active principle that calls itself Life has adapted itself even to this form. All other expressions lie in a winter sleep, life is simply one continual watch against the menace of death;—it has transformed us into unthinking animals in order to give us the weapon of instinct—it has reinforced us with dullness, so that we do not go to pieces before the horror ... it has lent us the indifference of wild creatures ..."— Remarque (1929) 163.

The whole question of motivation becomes moot. There is no rational motive for the warriors to be where they are. Helen is nothing to Ulysses. When force has stripped the soul of an expectation that things can be different, the will to live fades away in a pervasive desire to kill the enemy. War acquires its own momentum. Weil (1962b) 269: "Sacrifices already incurred are a perpetual argument for new ones. Thus there would never be any reason to stop killing and dying, except that there is fortunately a limit to human endurance." Robbed of even the instinct to survive, the victims of force constitute a species apart. Given the utter lack of hope for himself, how can the warrior be expected to countenance such a hope in another? Lycaon appealing to Achilles might as well be asking for a suspension of the order of nature. Why complain? asks Achilles: we all die. Patroclus alone, in the *Iliad*, is capable of human sympathy. All others are reduced to elemental energy, no more caring than wind or fire.

47. Force is external to all men, whether they seem to be its users or its objects. In the passage quoted from Book 24, the apparently victorious Achilles realizes that force has deprived his own father, Peleus, of his son just as surely as Priam has been deprived of Hector. Cf. Richardson (1993) 332–33: "In Greek society failure to care for one's parents in old age has always been regarded as one of the worst faults. Here it is even worse for Akhilleus, since he is not only unable to look after Peleus, but is forced to waste his life at Troy, giving trouble to Priam and his children." Also Macleod (1982) 134: "It is a fine touch that Achilles sees both Priam's and Peleus' suffering as embodied in one and the same person: himself. This reinforces the argument that the two old men's misfortunes are equal; and it brings out how detached Achilles is from his role as warrior."

48. As for the possibility of evading the dire effects of force, Weil argues that a "magnificent indifference" blinds the users of force to the claims of their fellow men. This was something she had also learned from Thucydides, who, in the Melian Dialogue, makes the Athenians assert that "it is a necessity of nature ... that each one, whether god or man, exercises all the power at his disposal" (Thuc. 5.105.2), "like the expansion of a gas in the *entire* space lying open to it"—Weil (1956b) 182, cf. 198, and Pétrement (1976) 350–51. Force, like Boyle's Law, is amoral. In Book 9, for example,

Achilles, in responding to the high command's efforts to secure his return, states the realities of the risk involved with cool objectivity. Nothing is worth more to him than his life. Not all of Troy may bring back a life once it is lost. Cf. Hainsworth (1993) 115–16: "Honour ... may draw death's sting but is not an equivalent for life on any rational calculation. Only Akhilleus in his splendid isolation from the ties of family and community can make such a point."

49. No one, however, will listen—the level heads (Odysseus, Phoenix, Ajax) sent in Book 9 to persuade Achilles to re-enter the war certainly are not convinced. And should an inferior propose a moderate course of action, he is simply beaten down, like Thersites in Book 2. The gods intervene to block reasonable behavior. Weil probably has in mind such episodes as Hera and Athena thwarting the potential peace in Book 4.1–104, when Pandarus is prompted to break the truce after the duel of Menelaus and Paris. But to attribute the mindless continuation of war to the gods is tantamount to admitting the true cause is unknown; nor do we in modern times have any better explanation. Weil (1962b) 270: "Nowadays the popular mind has an explanation for this sombre zeal in piling up useless ruin; it imagines the machinations of economic interests.... The truth is that the role which we attribute to mysterious economic oligarchies was attributed by Homer's contemporaries to the gods of Greek mythology. But there is no need of gods or conspiracies to make men rush headlong into the most absurd disasters. Human nature suffices." Thus, when he rebukes the despairing Agamemnon in Book 14, Odysseus alludes almost in passing to the inevitable destruction of warriors as taken for granted by all participants in war. Cf. Schein (1984) 72: "The fact that 'each of us' ["to the last man"] will perish through the very warfare that makes life meaningful indicates the costs as well as the rewards of the heroism Homer celebrates...."

50. Weil alludes to Craonne, the site of intensive fighting during World War I. She was familiar with a "Chanson de Craonne" that Paul Vaillant-Courturier had recorded in 1917 during the Nivelle offensive. In particular, she quoted the refrain "Car nous sommes tous condamnés/ Nous sommes les sacrifiés" ["Since we are all condemned/ We are the sacrificed"]—see Weil (1989) 320, n. 224. Craonne had also been the site of bloody battle a century earlier (7

March 1814) during Napoleon's desperate final efforts before the fall of Paris and his abdication. The French lost some 5,000 men, Blücher an equal number, as, "a professional soldier to the end, Napoleon led a military forlorn hope against immense odds, and prolonged a useless struggle beyond expectation"—Thompson (1951) 252. Regarding Weil's notion of warriors sensing that they are "the condemned," cf. Remarque (1929) 162: "It is a great brotherhood, which to a condition of life arising out of the midst of danger, out of the tension and forlornness of death, adds something of the good-fellowship of the folk-song, of the feeling of solidarity of convicts, and of the desperate loyalty to one another of men condemned to death...."

51. Men do not go off to war with such a grimly fatal outlook, however. In the jubilant mood of a large well-armed body of men as yet unopposed by an enemy, soldiers actually delight in a sense of adventure and in a false opinion of their freedom of will. Weil may be thinking of the mood of soldiers setting out for war in 1914; cf. Garraty and Gay (1972) 981: "With what innocence, with what enthusiasm, did the Europeans of 1914 respond to the tocsin!... [They] marched off to battle with something close to exultation, proud in their patriotism and certain of their cause, confident of a victorious end in a short time." In *Iliad* 8, when the army has lost faith in itself, Agamemnon caustically recalls to the Greeks their high spirits at Lemnos just before they landed at Troy. Cf. Wilson (1996) 191: "This is one of Agamemnon's few contributions to the action of this book, and it does nothing to dispel the impression of a maladroit and self-centred leader that we have already received from the previous books."

52. In the early stages of hostilities, too, men may sustain the illusion of sport and adventure, especially if they are momentarily successful. There is a quality of theater or sport about it all, as the heroes play their positions on the battlefield oblivious of imminent danger. Cf. Fussell (1989) 52: "War must rely on the young, for only they have the two things fighting requires: physical stamina and innocence about their own mortality. The young are proud of their athleticism, and because their sense of honor has not yet suffered compromise, they make the most useful material for manning the sharp end of war. Knowledge will come after a

few months, and then they'll be used up and as soldiers virtually useless—scared, cynical, debilitated, unwilling."

53. This *joie de combattre* is short lived. No war is continuous triumph. The warrior soon tastes fear and defeat, sees beloved friends die in battle, learns that his own death, too, is inevitable. Cf. Shay (1994) 39: "We often hear that the death of a special friend-in-arms broke the survivor's life into unhealable halves, with everything before his death radically severed from everything after." All hopes for the future vanish before the inescapable and vivid presentiment of death that he must face each morning. In the words of a veteran of Ypres in 1917, "The morrow! My heart stood still at the thought. [The] last hours before a battle were always the most torturing.... If only some alternative were open. But I knew that I had no choice—and I could see no valid reason why I should again escape mutilation or death"—Gladden (1967) 127, quoted in Fussell (1975) 171. Cf. O'Brien (1990) 21, on the same circumstances in Vietnam: "Each morning, despite the unknowns, they made their legs move. They endured. They kept humping. They did not submit to the obvious alternative, which was simply to close the eyes and fall." The soul is violated, mutilated irreparably, so that it can neither effect nor even imagine an exit from the realm of force. Many combatants in the First World War came to disbelieve that the war might ever have an end: "One did not have to be a lunatic or a particularly despondent visionary to conceive quite seriously that the war would never end and become a permanent condition of mankind.... Why not indeed, given the palpable irrationality of the new world?"—Fussell (1975) 71. This grim awareness of unending horror is the "yoke of warfare," which force has made a necessity. Weil takes the imagery from Aeschylus, who symbolizes the Greek concept of *ananke* as a yoke-strap or harness; see, e.g., Aeschylus, *Agamemnon* 218–21: "And when he [Agamemnon] had put on the yoke-strap of compulsion [ἐπεὶ δ' ἀνάγκας ἔδυ λέπαδνον],/ his spirit's wind veering to an impious blast,/ impure, unholy, from that moment/ his mind changed to a temper of utter ruthlessness"—trans. Lloyd-Jones (1979) 28.

54. Even should the soul long for deliverance, it cannot bear that the price already exacted by force should be for naught. The warrior becomes compulsive, like a gambler, recklessly hoping to recoup

losses but only adding to them. Weil (1962b) 269: "No one felt that the cost [of the war] was too great, because they were all in pursuit of a literal non-entity whose only value was the price paid for it." Athena reminds Odysseus of this consideration in Book 2, and we find him still using it to spur on Agamemnon in Book 14. On this sort of "sunk-costs argument," see Shay (1994) 157–58, and Nevin (1991) 115: "Odysseus argues that the war against Troy must go on because so many have died in it. Weil saw precisely the same rationale in Poincaré's conduct during the Great War. Peacemaking, short of total military victory, would betray the dead."

55. War is irrational; there can be no true justification for taking part in it. In Weil's memorable question, "What is Helen to Ulysses?" (Though she does not allude to it, there was a tradition that Odysseus attempted to "dodge the draft" before the war: see the summary of the *Cypria*, a Cyclic Epic, in Evelyn-White [1936] 492–93.) The men fight on but not for any adequate compensation that the fall of Troy might bring. Weil (1962b) 269: "The Greeks and Trojans massacred one another for ten years on account of Helen. Not one of them except the dilettante warrior Paris cared two straws about her.... The person of Helen was obviously out of scale with this gigantic struggle that in the eyes of all she was no more than the symbol of what was really at stake; but the real issue was never defined by anyone, nor could it be, because it did not exist." The maimed souls of the warriors simply thirst for annihilation, both others' and their own. As we see in Book 18, Achilles, after the loss of his cherished Patroclus, would like nothing more than to die himself. Cf. Shay (1994) 52: "Homer affirms that Achilles is 'already dead'.... Words and conventional gestures associated with mourning the dead are used in reference to Achilles...." As so often, Homer is depicting experiences common to other wars in other places: cf. Shay, ibid.: "Speaking of the time after his closest friend-in-arms was killed, a [Vietnam] veteran said: 'And it wasn't that I couldn't be killed. I didn't *care* if I was killed.... I just didn't care if I lived or died. I just wanted blood. I just wanted revenge, and I didn't care. I didn't see myself going home. No ... nope ... no, I didn't'"; also Caputo (1977) 247–48: "Thousands of people died each week in the war, and the sum of all their deaths did not make any difference.... My death would

not alter a thing. Walking down the trail, I could not remember having felt an emotion more sublime or liberating than that indifference toward my own death."

56. Thus, it deters Achilles not one whit to learn (repeatedly from his mother, Thetis, and others: 18.95–96, cf. 19.409–17) that his own life will be forfeit if he takes the field to exact vengeance from Hector. He wants the grim satisfaction of giving the Trojans their fill of war. Cf. Schadewaldt (1997b) 156: "Something like an atmosphere of death overshadows this scene in which Achilles commits himself to revenge and his own destruction ..."; Zanker (1994) 100: "Death has totally lost relevance to his decision-making processes."

57. Such a man, with such motivations, is no longer a member of the species of the living. Though he has come to it by a different path, he is like the suppliant or the slave in having reached the piteous bastard status of a "living thing." Cf. Shay (1994) 51: "'I died in Vietnam' is a common utterance of our [chronic post-traumatic stress disorder] patients. Most viewed themselves as already dead at some point in their combat service, often after a close friend was killed."

58. Given the "victor's" abolition of all aspirations, save death, the appeal of a suppliant (Weil returns to the Lycaon episode in Book 21) is a waste of breath. Cf. Owen (1946) 208: "This pathetic figure, with his pitiable story and his childish plea that he is only half-brother to Hector ... if he cannot win mercy from Achilles, we get a dreadful foretaste of what the meeting with Hector will be like. The poet is giving us a glimpse into the black hate that has filled Achilles' heart"; Segal (1971) 49: "Achilles, having given up his own hold on life, could not respect life in another."

59. Achilles, who obsessively foresees, and even craves, his own death, answers Lycaon with supreme resignation. Far better men than Lycaon have succumbed to force, and will yet succumb; to protest the end assigned us all is as pointless as it is spineless. Cf. Griffin (1980) 55: "Achilles kills in a passionate revenge, but not in blind ferocity. He sees his action in the perspective of human life and death as a whole, the perspective which puts slayer and slain on a level, so that it is more than a mere colloquialism that he calls Lykaon 'friend' as he kills him"; so too Schein (1984) 98–99, Knox (1990) 37: "that macabre word 'friend' is sincerely meant ...," and

Postlethwaite (2000) 259–60. But contrast Shay (1994) 94: "Achilles is so cut off from human compassion that he even addresses Lykaôn as 'friend' (*phílos*) as he tells him that the only possible community between them is that of death—and executes him. This so-called 'consolation' to Lykaôn is nothing but the chilling cruelty of the berserker; a warmer reading of this scene is ruled out by Achilles' gratuitous mistreatment and mocking of Lykaôn's corpse."

60. For an individual mired in the dominion of force, subject to its soul-diminishing influence, to appreciate another's desire for life requires almost superhuman altruism. Indeed, Weil remarks, few men in history have possessed it. Force renders deaf and speech-less nearly all whom it touches, transforms them into "plagues of nature," no more amenable to words of petition than a disease would be. Only Patroclus is an exception in the *Iliad*. Though a most formidable warrior, he also has the capacity for kindness; cf. Edwards (1991) 127: "He is the only person to whom μείλιχος ["gentle"] is applied, here [17.671] and when Briseis says that he was μείλιχος αἰεί ["always gentle"] (19.300; it is used with a negative for Hektor by Andromakhe, 24.739). Patroklos' gentle-ness is unique in the language of the poem...." See, too, Shay (1994) 46: "Homer asks us to believe that gentleness and compas-sion really were Patroklos's leading character traits, equal to his fighting prowess against the enemy. If we fail to perceive this, we will be unable to comprehend the pain at his death."

Paragraphs 61–62

The nature of force—its property of "petrifying" both users and vic-tims—is, of course, painfully apparent in the crucible of war. The resolution of a battle is not brought about by rational calculation, stra-tegic planning, or tactical maneuvers. It is a plain case of mass versus mass, force in collision with force. Weil notes that this is the net effect of the famous similes of the *Iliad*. Men are consistently compared with elements—earth, air, fire, and water—or with animals. War is sym-bolically and literally a process of metamorphosis. The souls of the combatants are the casualties of this dreadful alchemy overseen by the Homeric gods.

61. As Weil restates the theme of force as petrifactive, she observes that the decision of battles is a function of brute force, of inert mass opposed to inert mass. She may have in mind Tolstoy's notion of men at war as mindlessly unreflective; see, for example, *War and Peace*, Book 9, chap. 1, on Napoleon's Russian campaign of 1812: "Millions of men, renouncing their human feelings and reason, had to go from west to east to slay their fellows, just as some centuries previously hordes of men had come from the east to the west slaying their fellows" (trans. Maude and Maude [1933]). She next asserts that the *Iliad* conveys this by its similes. The famous Homeric similes (there are over 300 in the *Iliad*) have been the subject of many studies. They are often said to serve a "relieving" function, taking the reader for a moment out of the brutality of war to the world of peace and nature. Weil insists that most serve rather to enhance our impression of the dehumanizing impact of force. In the images of the similes, men are metaphorically changed into inert matter, elemental forces, or animals. In the simile from Book 15, Hector is metamorphosed into a lion. In the one quoted from Book 11, Agamemnon is no longer even sentient—he is fire; elsewhere in the same book, Hector is "like a whirlwind" (11.297–98) and "like a thunderstorm" (11.305–9). On similes in Homer generally, see Fränkel (1997), Lee (1964), Nimis (1987), Edwards (1991) 24–41, Clarke (1995), and commentary on para. 34, above.

62. War is thus the art of transformations. Human beings, it appears, are quite mutable, susceptible to profound alterations in their mode of existence, alterations brought by force on the authority of—for lack of a better explanation—the gods. The petrified human soul itself is the true object of war. Only rarely does it escape the consequences of an individual's contact with force. Cf. the Vietnam war veteran quoted in Shay (1994) 83: "December 22, 1967, is the day the civilized me became an animal.... I was a fucking animal. When I look back at that stuff, I say, 'That was somebody else that did that. Wasn't me. That wasn't me.... Who the fuck was that?'... War changes you ... strips you of all your beliefs, your religion, takes your dignity away, you become an animal."

Paragraphs 63–71

The world picture of the *Iliad* as Weil has outlined it to this point is
unremittingly bleak. But, she points out, there are moments of illumination or deliverance, in which human beings cease to be inanimate.
In these moments when the soul awakens, love is not unknown in the
epic.

Weil itemizes several sorts of love or, more broadly, human at-
tachment: the guest-host relation, the love of kin, of friends, and—
most miraculously—even of enemies. Weil speaks of these as "moments of grace"; that is, in her theological vocabulary (developed in
Weil [1952a]), moments of exemption from the "gravity" of necessity,
of deliverance from the harsh realities that enmesh the soul and prevent its reaching the heights humanity at its best is capable of. The
sense of potential shut off, of the soul oppressed, of what might have
been, is what makes the domain of force so terrible.

63. Weil now steps back a bit from the prosecution of her argument
    that force is the true hero of the poem and observes that Homer
    has relieved the gloom by including some few moments of grace,
    when men act out of love rather than hate. In these moments of
    reflection and insight, the soul awakens and shows itself capable
    of pure courage and love. Weil refers to the interior monologue of
    Hector alone outside the walls, exposed to the coming onslaught,
    as he assesses his own motivations and shrinking prospects (see
    para. 43).
64. The next example Weil gives is the guest-host relation, *xenia*
    (ξενία), sanctified by Zeus and dear to Homer the story-teller (no-
    tably in the *Odyssey*). Though largely a matter of good form and
    not of attachment stemming from deep mutual affinity, the code
    of *xenia* is still compelling enough to interrupt the mayhem of
    combat. In the lines quoted from Book 6, we see the enduring
    strength of this tie in the separate peace of Diomedes and Glau-
    cus, who perpetuate a bond begun by their grandfathers.
65. The love of parent for child is apparent every time the long-
    suffering Thetis appears in the epic. The lines Weil cites are from a
    conversation in which Thetis both tries to console Achilles as he
    laments Patroclus and herself grieves at her son's decision to enter
    battle and thus hasten his own end. Cf. Owen (1946) 179: "Thetis's

coming also reminds us of Achilles' approaching death. As always, she brings the thought with her."

66. The love of the captive Briseis for her brothers has survived even her enslavement, though it may be given expression only here in the general context of mourning for Patroclus in Book 19. (See commentary on para. 19.)

67. The mutual devotion of Hector and Andromache is stressed in the poem. They are one another's all, in Andromache's case, literally so: Hector has taken the place in her heart of her lost father, mother, and seven brothers (6.414–30)! Cf. Edwards (1987) 209: "On the wider scale, it depicts the leave-taking at the onset of battle that took place time and again, year after year, in Greek families at every age and at all times and places since. No comparable examples of leave-takings are found in surviving ancient literature, but the frequency with which these scenes occur in Greek vase painting indicates their appeal."

68. The scenes between husband and wife earlier, in Book 6, heighten the pathos of Andromache's final lament in Book 24. There was for her no final consoling word to cling to in facing a bleak future. Cf. Macleod (1982) 149: "In 6.450–65, Hector predicted Andromache's future: here she does so herself. In 6.476–81, Hector fondly imagined that Astyanax would live to be a better warrior than his father: here Andromache guesses the truth, that he will be killed in his babyhood because of his father's prowess in war. Thus the Trojan episode of Book 6, so far from being a mere interlude, creates a tension which sustains the poem to its end...."

69. And, of course, the love between Achilles and Patroclus is stronger even than blood. Cf. Achilles' prayer at 16.97–100: "Father Zeus, Athene, and Apollo, if only/ not one of all the Trojans could escape destruction, not one/ of the Argives, but you and I could emerge from the slaughter/ so that we two alone could break Troy's hallowed coronal" (trans. Lattimore [1951]). The behavior of the disconsolate Achilles after Patroclus' death is eloquent testimony to the depth of his love. His "sleeplessness springs from emotional turmoil, not merely watchful concern" — Macleod (1982) 85. Achilles will even knowingly barter his own life to avenge his dead friend.

70. The "supreme grace" is the love of an enemy. Weil no doubt alludes to Matt. 5:43–44: "You have heard that they were told, 'Love

your neighbor and hate your enemy.' But what I tell you is this: Love your enemies and pray for your persecutors." It is just this that crowns the *Iliad* with moments of sublimity during the interview of Achilles and Priam in Book 24. Cf. Griffin (1980) 16: "He treats his guest with courtesy and eats with him, then they gaze at each other and admire in each other the nobility and beauty which each possesses. This has given the poet here a metaphor which enables Achilles to return to humanity before he meets his death."

71. Homer has relieved his depressing history of force but also brought home to us the losses that war causes. The *Iliad* provides a precious few glimpses of what human beings might be, were the sway of force less oppressive, vicious, and universal. Cf. Macleod (1982) 26–27: "Achilles' love for his friend is one source of his sympathy for Priam, no longer just a cause for hatred and rage against the Trojans.... In short, ambition, vindictiveness and resentment all give way to pity. The war will go on, with Achilles taking part; and even now his anger is not far away. But here Achilles is clinging to his kinder, not his fiercer self...."

Paragraphs 72–79

The *Iliad* might easily have become an unendurably forbidding and repellent work. It is redeemed, however, by its tone of regret at all human suffering. The poet does not revel in the triumph of victors, since there are no true victors in the world of his poem, nor does he glory over the defeated enemy. The plight of Trojan warriors, from minor ones to Hector himself, is depicted with great sympathy. No man's pain is undervalued. The attitude of the poet and consequently of his readers is one of compassion: the people of the epic carry a burden of anguish typical of the human condition. In this respect, we and they are kin.

The overriding mood of regret in the *Iliad* stems naturally from its subject—the loss of a city. (In 1940, the destruction of Warsaw and the fall of Paris were painfully immediate instances of what Weil calls "the worst of human hardships.") Brief, lovingly detailed evocations of earlier days of peace intensify our feelings of loss and grief at devastation that will escalate to an unimaginable pitch with the fall of

Troy. The untempered fury of war is thrust in our faces. The warriors caught up in its machinery are neither admirable nor contemptible. They are all victims of force, horrible mutants transformed by an amoral destiny to which we are all subject.

72. The claim that the *Iliad* is saved by bitterness from being a cold and gruesome rehearsal of violent acts may seem paradoxical. "Bitterness" for Weil was a state of higher awareness and sensitivity reached only through hardship, as in the Aeschylean formula "learning through suffering" (e.g., Aeschylus, *Agamemnon* 177). Cf. Weil (1956b) 258: "Just as one consents to one's own affliction when it comes upon one, so one must consent to that of others when it is *absolutely* impossible to prevent it, but with the same irreducible bitterness. This bitterness does not prevent the love of God, for it does not prevent one from feeling beauty; it is, rather, a precondition for feeling it. It is through this bitterness that the *Iliad* is beautiful. There is no first-class art without this core of bitterness." Because we see force unjustly exposing men and women like ourselves to pain and death, the events of the epic are paradoxically bathed in a light of justice and love. The poem evokes pity for all victims, but perhaps most sharply for the enemy: Weil's first example, the Trojan Iphidamas, is likely chosen for the detail that he is a newlywed. Agamemnon, in the frenzy of his *aristeia*, kills this young warrior, who leaves behind his bride "and had known no delight from her yet, and given much for her" (11.243, trans. Lattimore [1951]). Cf. Griffin (1980) 134: "The particular interest of this passage is the explicit epithet οἰκτρός 'pitiable' [*malheureux* in Weil]; the poet himself gives utterance to the pity he feels for the unlucky young husband."

73. Weil's second example of a Trojan whose misfortune touches our hearts is again the luckless Lycaon, who enjoyed only eleven days out of captivity before the gods delivered him once more to Achilles, this time to the final captivity of death. Cf. Postlethwaite (2000) 258: "Lykaon is one of a rare breed, a warrior who has encountered Achilleus and lived: his experience recalls a time when Achilleus took pity on prisoners ..., so his treatment here is a measure of the change Achilleus has undergone."

74. Next there is Menelaus slaying comely Euphorbus, who had wounded Patroclus shortly before (again the seesaw of war). Cf.

Edwards (1991) 68: "The unusual description of Euphorbos' finery
… emphasizes the contrast between his pride and his fall. The defiling with blood and dust of a dead warrior's hair is repeated at
the death of Hektor" (and see para. 3). The text does not support
Weil's statement that Euphorbus "had seen only one day of war":
though he appears in the poem only on this day of Patroclus'
death, Homer notes that he is a veteran who had slain twenty men
before his greatest triumph—the wounding of Patroclus (see
16.806–15).

75. Then there is Hector, whose demise in itself is pitiable, but whose
loss spells death for "chaste wives and small children" as well. As
Hector runs his race of life and death, Homer, by a sudden reference to the place of the washerwomen, adroitly accentuates the
tension between the present bloody contests of warriors and the
everyday domestic activities in long-gone times of peace in the
same locales.

76. Even though it is the "enemy's" city, we are made to feel the supreme misery of Troy's destruction. But Homer also evokes sympathy for the momentarily victorious Greeks, many of whom
perish far from home.

77. In Book 11, another evocation of a humble peacetime routine—the
lunch-hour of the woodcutter—amplifies the abnormal normality
of the warriors' work. In the workaday world of war, they cut
down men as if they were trees; again, we witness the "blind indifference" that force instills. Postlethwaite (2000) 155 notes that
the image "calls attention to the Achaians' heightened aggression,
for they increase their efforts at the time the woodcutter relaxes
from his."

78. Homer consistently magnifies the shocking disparity between war
and peace. The images of peace are adorned with an all-too-fragile
tranquillity and nostalgia, while those of war are presented un-
varnished, as in the passage from Book 16, which graphically
depicts Idomeneus killing the Trojan nonentity, Erymas, whose
"vivid death should scare us as well as the Trojans"—Janko (1992)
361. Cf. O'Brien (1990) 13, 17: "right then Ted Lavender was shot
in the head…. He lay with his mouth open. The teeth were broken. There was a swollen black bruise under his left eye. The
cheekbone was gone…. Like cement, Kiowa whispered in the
dark. I swear to God—boom, down. Not a word."

79. On the neutrality of Homer and of Zeus, see Introduction, p. 9, and commentary on para. 32 above. Nonetheless, Homer's gods succeed, as promoters of force, in catalyzing the degradation of humans into animals or inert matter.

Paragraphs 80–83

Weil now argues that the Greeks were virtually alone in the production of a literature based on a fair and sympathetic assessment of the value and common lot of all humankind. She focuses more narrowly on a theme developed in the course of her essay—the impartiality of the *Iliad*. She has taken pains to prove that Homer does not champion the Greek cause and in fact portrays Greeks and Trojans with equal sympathy. She now suggests a possible explanation: the Achaeans the poet of the *Iliad* sang for and about had experienced both victory (in the Trojan War) and defeat (during the Dorian Invasion); they had seen war and its outcomes from both sides.

Weil observes again the remarkable bitterness (see commentary on para. 72) or resigned recognition through suffering that imbues the epic with an impartial love for all human beings as they undergo the devastations of force. Few other works of literature exhibit such lack of bias in gauging the worth of one's fellow human beings, in recognizing their all-too-human susceptibility to force, and in loving them both despite and because of their vulnerability. After Homer, says Weil, only Greek tragedy and the Gospels measure up to this standard of insight.

Weil distills the issues raised in the *Iliad* in her own special moral and aesthetic terminology. The question of the soul's affliction by "necessity" (involvement in force and matter) is paramount; how far may "grace" (the spiritual "lightness" which alone releases one from the gravity of necessity) preserve the soul from the temptations force poses in all its manifestations? Can the human spirit resist the urge to hate, to degrade, to be indifferent? The Greeks alone seem to have given us a literature that inculcates essential lessons for the living of a just life, filled with awareness of the common predicament of humankind.

80. The historical reconstruction Weil gives here, with an admission that it can be no more than sheer speculation, runs as follows: victors in the Trojan War (traditionally ca. 1184 B.C.), the Achaeans, according to Greek historical tradition (cf. Thucydides 1.12), in their own turn suffered conquest and exile eastward across the Aegean — to the area where Homer later lived and composed his epics — during the so-called "Dorian Invasion" (traditionally ca. 1100 B.C.). Since iron was in Greece a post-invasion technology and is almost unknown in Homer, the origins of the *Iliad*, Weil argues, may indeed date to the transitional age between bronze and iron, not long after the fall of Troy. The epic's creator and his audience had, therefore, attained their impartiality by hard experience: they (or their ancestors) had both taken and lost cities, and had known the pain of life "far from their homeland" (for the phrase, τηλόθι πάτρης, see, e.g., 1.30 or 18.99). For current scholarly opinion on these matters, see Latacz (1996) 23–69 and idem (2001). Assessments of Homer's disinterest as opposed to "national bias" have reached differing conclusions: see, e.g., Mackie (1996) 6–10 and *passim*.

81. Whatever the historical causes of it may have been, the *Iliad* displays a nearly unique insight into human life. Specifically, all men alike are subject to the "gravity" or force of matter. The poet of the *Iliad* had the remarkable ability to see this truth and to fashion his epic accordingly. Cf. Shay (1994) 118: "Homer is not a propagandist for either Greeks or Trojans, and he does not dehumanize the warriors of either side, inflaming our emotions against them as evil monsters or subhuman vermin." No other European epic matches up: even Homer's own *Odyssey* seems a poor replica of the *Iliad* or of "oriental" poems (such as the *Gilgamesh* epic). Weil finds the *Aeneid*, as she finds all things Roman, unfeeling and artificial, particularly in comparison with the *Iliad*. And the *Chanson de Roland* is marred for her by an egregious bias in favor of Christian heroes against the "infidel" Saracens.

82. Aeschylus, Sophocles, and the Evangelists (especially in the Passion narrative) were for Weil the only writers able to approach the wisdom of the *Iliad*. (The injunction "seek the kingdom ..." is from Matt. 6:33.) She strives to make a case for the Gospels as imbued with the Greek genius. For her, the agony and death of Christ symbolize the conditions of all life on earth. God, like all our

souls, was afflicted by the gravity that works on all flesh. The pain he underwent in Gethsemane and on the cross was a metaphoric version of the plight of all human beings; Weil (1970) 337–38: "Christ on the cross had compassion for his own suffering, as being the suffering of humanity in him. His cry: 'My God, why hast thou forsaken me?' [Matt. 27:46 = Mark 15:34] was the cry of all men in him. When that cry rises in a man's heart, pain has awoken in the depths of his soul the part where there dwells, buried under sins, an innocence equal to Christ's own." In Weil's view, the compassion of God for man was emulated in the world view of the *Iliad*. All its characters, however brutal their behavior, however many their sins, possessed a fundamental innocence. The ability to love one's fellow man, she argues, is predicated on an awareness of the suffering to which force subjects us all, without exception. All the warriors are united in their liability to its universal effects. In arguing that both the *Iliad* and the Gospels share this common insight of the Greek genius, Weil even points out a verbal similarity between *Iliad* 21.48 (Lycaon) and John 21:18 (Christ to Peter).

83. In Weil's theology, the world in which the soul finds itself is necessarily subject to chance; the gods are impartial, and destiny will take its course oblivious to divine or human volition. In such a context, it is an open question how far grace may insulate the soul from the symptoms of its corruption: arrogance, contempt for one's fellows, plain indifference. For Weil, the Greeks alone had the rare capacity to understand all this and to depict the lot of human beings honestly.

Paragraphs 84–86

Simone Weil held inflexible opinions regarding literature and, concomitantly, the people who produced a given literature. On the one hand, the Greeks are for her the best, because, as she has contended in the previous four paragraphs, their literary tradition shows a remarkable appreciation of the true situation of men and women in the world of force. On the other, the Romans and the Hebrews are castigated for having no such appreciation of things as they are. The Romans held a notion of manifest destiny that they felt immunized them against the damage of force and entitled them to wield it with impunity against all non-Romans. The result was blood sports, not great epics. The Hebrews, believing themselves to be the "Chosen People," likewise felt authorized by their God to inflict pain on the non-Chosen. The result was, except perhaps for the Book of Job and a few other passages, a scriptural tradition that is "a tissue of horrors" (Weil [1965] 160), endorsing cruelty to the enemy and contempt for the unfortunate. With her lifelong propensity to suffer in sympathy with the downtrodden, Weil could not abide any claim that some people deserved to be harmed or destroyed. She never misses an opportunity to attack Roman and Hebrew literature for their (in her view) disgraceful incomprehension of the true nature of force.

Christianity, too, Weil contends, has been contaminated by false assumptions regarding the pervasive anguish that force causes. Martyrs were thought to be exempt from the torments that Christ himself experienced. And the Church perverted its mission by wielding force in its own interest to coerce conversions to the faith.

The Greek genius for understanding the plight of all men has, with a few exceptions, vanished from European literature. Whether that understanding can be recaptured, Weil concludes, remains to be seen. Cf. Bertrand Russell on the frustrations of his attempts to awaken the world to the apocalyptically lethal force of atomic weapons: "Whether mankind will think itself worth preserving remains a doubtful question"—Russell (1969) 222.

84. Weil detested Rome and the Romans. She felt the *Aeneid* was a cold, insincere, contrived work, in large part because of its propagation of the Roman myth of manifest destiny. The gods of Vergil sanction and approve the Roman mission of conquest and world dominion. "We are right, all others wrong." So too, the Hebrews, as self-styled "Chosen People," were blinded by pride; Weil (1970) 297: "The virtue of humility is incompatible with the sense of belonging to a social group chosen by God, whether a nation (Hebrews, Romans, Germans, etc.) or a Church." On the notion of one's enemies as "repellent to God himself," see Shay (1994) 103: "[In] Vietnam-era military training ... the enemy soldier was depicted as evil and loathsome, deserving to be killed as the enemy of God.... By contrast, the *Iliad* emphatically portrays the enemy as worthy of respect, even honor" (cf. idem 111–15 on the biblical

story of David and Goliath as illustrative of the tendency to de-humanize the enemy). Thus, for Weil, the sins of nationalism, fanaticism, and cruelty in the name of a higher cause have always been justified by appeal to the precedents of the Romans and He-brews, who lacked the indispensable consciousness of kinship with those who suffer. That sense of affiliation was a dominant feature of Weil's own life: "The suffering all over the world ob-sesses me and overwhelms me to the point of annihilating my faculties, and the only way I can revive them and release myself from the obsession is by getting for myself a large share of danger and hardship"—letter to Maurice Schumann, quoted in Pétrement (1976) 482. Hence her (never-realized) schemes to form a front-line nursing corps or join the Resistance inside occupied France: see Pétrement (1976) 374–75, 514.

85. Even the Gospels, those last representatives of the Greek genius, have been polluted through the centuries by mistaken ideas of the effects of force—notions deriving from Rome and Israel; Weil (1965) 129–30 [(1977) 83]: "I have never been able to understand how it is possible for a reasonable mind to regard the Jehovah of the Bible and the Father who is invoked in the Gospels as one and the same being. The influence of the Old Testament and of the Roman Empire, whose tradition was continued in the Papacy, are to my mind the two essential sources of the corruption of Christi-anity." Christians have been wrong to think grace could inoculate one against suffering: the martyrs did not have a grace that Christ lacked. The soul may indeed survive but not without the wound of ultimate understanding of man's lot in the kingdom of force. The Church even applied force to convert others, believing itself to be acting righteously.

86. Weil concludes with a dark estimate of European literature, which has revived the spirit of the Greek genius only sporadically in Vil-lon, Shakespeare, Cervantes, Molière, Racine, and possibly a few others. (On relevant passages in Molière [L'Ecole des femmes 1024] and Racine [Phèdre 191–94], see Weil [1989] 321, nn. 259–60.) She contends we will continue to labor under dangerous delusions about the nature of force and the human predicament until that spirit is recovered. Well might she say in 1940 that "It is doubtful whether this will soon occur." Well may we still today.

Appendix

Simone Weil quotes some 250 lines of Homer's *Iliad*: "The translation of cited passages is new. Each line renders one Greek verse, with caesuras and enjambments scrupulously reproduced. The word order within each verse has also been respected as far as possible"—Weil (1989) 227. To facilitate comparison of her careful renditions with their originals, I have given below the Greek text of every passage quoted in the essay. The text adopted is the bilingual "Budé edition" by Paul Mazon et al., *Homère: Iliade*, 4 vols. (Paris: Société d'Édition "Les Belles Lettres," 1937–1938). Though Weil does not specify this edition, we know that she was familiar with it from her critique of the French translation in a letter to Jean Posternak. (See Introduction, n. 16, and Weil [1989] 318–19, n. 163.) Mazon's text is virtually identical to that of the widely available Oxford Classical Text edition: D.B. Munro and T.W. Allen, eds., *Homeri Opera*, vols. 1-2, 3rd ed. (Oxford: Clarendon Press, 1920).

~ô ~ô ~ô

Para.   … ἵπποι
2   κείν' ὄχεα κροτάλιζον ἀνὰ πτολέμοιο γεφύρας,
     ἡνιόχους ποθέοντες ἀμύμονας· οἱ δ' ἐπὶ γαίῃ
     κείατο, γύπεσσιν πολὺ φίλτεροι ἢ ἀλόχοισιν.

                                              11.159–62

3   … ἀμφὶ δὲ χαῖται
     κυάνεαι πίτναντο, κάρη δ' ἅπαν ἐν κονίῃσι

κεῖτο πάρος χαρίεν· τότε δὲ Ζεὺς δυσμενέεσσι
δῶκεν ἀεικίσσασθαι ἑῇ ἐν πατρίδι γαίῃ.

22.401–4

4   ψυχὴ δ' ἐκ ῥεθέων πταμένη Ἄιδος δὲ βεβήκει,
ὃν πότμον γοόωσα, λιποῦσ' ἀνδροτῆτα καὶ ἥβην.

22.362–63

5   Κέκλετο δ' ἀμφιπόλοισιν ἐυπλοκάμοις κατὰ δῶμα
ἀμφὶ πυρὶ στῆσαι τρίποδα μέγαν, ὄφρα πέλοιτο
Ἕκτορι θερμὰ λοετρὰ μάχης ἐκ νοστήσαντι,
νηπίη, οὐδ' ἐνόησεν ὅ μιν μάλα τῆλε λοετρῶν
χερσὶν Ἀχιλλῆος δάμασε γλαυκῶπις Ἀθήνη.

22.442–46

8   Ὣς ὥρμαινε μένων· ὁ δέ οἱ σχεδὸν ἦλθε τεθηπώς,
γούνων ἅψασθαι μεμαώς, περὶ δ' ἤθελε θυμῷ
ἐκφυγέειν θάνατόν τε κακὸν καὶ κῆρα μέλαιναν...
αὐτὰρ ὁ τῇ ἑτέρῃ μὲν ἑλὼν ἐλλίσσετο γούνων,
τῇ δ' ἑτέρῃ ἔχεν ἔγχος ἀκαχμένον οὐδὲ μεθίει ....

21.64–66, 71–72

9   Ὣς ἄρα μιν Πριάμοιο προσηύδα φαίδιμος υἱός
λισσόμενος ἐπέεσσιν, ἀμείλικτον δ' ὄπ' ἄκουσε ....
Ὣς φάτο, τοῦ δ' αὐτοῦ λύτο γούνατα καὶ φίλον ἦτορ·
ἔγχος μέν ῥ' ἀφέηκεν, ὁ δ' ἕζετο χεῖρε πετάσσας
ἀμφοτέρας· Ἀχιλεὺς δὲ ἐρυσσάμενος ξίφος ὀξὺ
τύψε κατὰ κληῖδα παρ' αὐχένα, πᾶν δέ οἱ εἴσω
δῦ ξίφος ἄμφηκες· ὁ δ' ἄρα πρηνὴς ἐπὶ γαίῃ
κεῖτο ταθείς, ἐκ δ' αἷμα μέλαν ῥέε, δεῦε δὲ γαῖαν.

21.97–98, 114–19

10   Τοὺς δ' ἔλαθ' εἰσελθὼν Πρίαμος μέγας, ἄγχι δ' ἄρα στὰς
χερσὶν Ἀχιλλῆος λάβε γούνατα καὶ κύσε χεῖρας
δεινὰς ἀνδροφόνους, αἵ οἱ πολέας κτάνον υἷας.

24.477–79

11 Ὡς δ' ὅτ' ἂν ἄνδρ' ἄτη πυκινὴ λάβῃ, ὅς τ' ἐνὶ πάτρῃ
φῶτα κατακτείνας ἄλλων ἐξίκετο δῆμον,
ἀνδρὸς ἐς ἀφνειοῦ, θάμβος δ' ἔχει εἰσορόωντας,
ὡς Ἀχιλεὺς θάμβησεν ἰδὼν Πρίαμον θεοειδέα·
θάμβησαν δὲ καὶ ἄλλοι, ἐς ἀλλήλους δὲ ἴδοντο.

24.480–84

12 Ὡς φάτο, τῷ δ' ἄρα πατρὸς ὑφ' ἵμερον ὦρσε γόοιο·
ἁψάμενος δ' ἄρα χειρὸς ἀπώσατο ἦκα γέροντα·
τὼ δὲ μνησαμένω, ὁ μὲν Ἕκτορος ἀνδροφόνοιο
κλαῖ' ἀδινὰ προπάροιθε ποδῶν Ἀχιλῆος ἐλυσθείς,
αὐτὰρ Ἀχιλλεὺς κλαῖεν ἑὸν πατέρ', ἄλλοτε δ' αὖτε
Πάτροκλον· τῶν δὲ στοναχὴ κατὰ δώματ' ὀρώρει.

24.507–12

13 Ὡς ἔφατ', ἔδδεισεν δ' ὁ γέρων καὶ ἐπείθετο μύθῳ.

24.571

15 τὴν δ' ἐγὼ οὐ λύσω· πρίν μιν καὶ γῆρας ἔπεισιν
ἡμετέρῳ ἐνὶ οἴκῳ, ἐν Ἄργεϊ, τηλόθι πάτρης,
ἱστὸν ἐποιχομένην καὶ ἐμὸν λέχος ἀντιόωσαν.

1.29–31

16 καί κεν ἐν Ἄργει ἐοῦσα πρὸς ἄλλης ἱστὸν ὑφαίνοις,
καί κεν ὕδωρ φορέοις Μεσσηίδος ἢ Ὑπερείης
πόλλ' ἀεκαζομένη, κρατερὴ δ' ἐπικείσετ' ἀνάγκη.

6.456–58

17 αἳ δή τοι τάχα νηυσὶν ὀχήσονται γλαφυρῇσι,
καὶ μὲν ἐγὼ μετὰ τῇσι· σὺ δ' αὖ, τέκος, ἢ ἐμοὶ αὐτῇ
ἕψεαι, ἔνθά κεν ἔργα ἀεικέα ἐργάζοιο,
ἀθλεύων πρὸ ἄνακτος ἀμειλίχου ....

24.731–34

19 Ὡς ἔφατο κλαίουσ', ἐπὶ δὲ στενάχοντο γυναῖκες,
Πάτροκλον πρόφασιν, σφῶν δ' αὐτῶν κήδε' ἑκάστη.

19.301–2

20   Ἄνδρα μὲν ᾧ ἔδοσάν με πατὴρ καὶ πότνια μήτηρ
εἶδον πρὸ πτόλιος δεδαϊγμένον ὀξέι χαλκῷ,
τρεῖς τε κασιγνήτους, τούς μοι μία γείνατο μήτηρ,
κηδείους, οἳ πάντες ὀλέθριον ἦμαρ ἐπέσπον.
Οὐδὲ μὲν οὐδέ μ' ἔασκες, ὅτ' ἄνδρ' ἐμὸν ὠκὺς Ἀχιλλεὺς
ἔκτεινεν, πέρσεν δὲ πόλιν θείοιο Μύνητος,
κλαίειν, ἀλλά μ' ἔφασκες Ἀχιλλῆος θείοιο
κουριδίην ἄλοχον θήσειν, ἄξειν δ' ἐνὶ νηυσὶν
ἐς Φθίην, δαίσειν δὲ γάμον μετὰ Μυρμιδόνεσσι·
τῶ σ' ἄμοτον κλαίω τεθνηότα, μείλιχον αἰεί.

                                    19.291–300

21   Καὶ γὰρ τ' ἠύκομος Νιόβη ἐμνήσατο σίτου,
τῇ περ δώδεκα παῖδες ἐνὶ μεγάροισιν ὄλοντο,
ἓξ μὲν θυγατέρες, ἓξ δ' υἱέες ἡβώοντες·
τοὺς μὲν Ἀπόλλων πέφνεν ἀπ' ἀργυρέοιο βιοῖο
χωόμενος Νιόβῃ, τὰς δ' Ἄρτεμις ἰοχέαιρα,
οὕνεκ' ἄρα Λητοῖ ἰσάσκετο καλλιπαρήῳ·
φῆ δοιὼ τεκέειν, ἡ δ' αὐτὴ γείνατο πολλούς·
τὼ δ' ἄρα καὶ δοιώ περ ἐόντ' ἀπὸ πάντας ὄλεσσαν.
Οἱ μὲν ἄρ' ἐννῆμαρ κέατ' ἐν φόνῳ, οὐδέ τις ἦεν
κατθάψαι, λαοὺς δὲ λίθους ποίησε Κρονίων·
τοὺς δ' ἄρα τῇ δεκάτῃ θάψαν θεοὶ Οὐρανίωνες·
ἡ δ' ἄρα σίτου μνήσατ', ἐπεὶ κάμε δάκρυ χέουσα.

                                    24.602–13

23   Δοιοὶ γάρ τε πίθοι κατακείαται ἐν Διὸς οὔδει
δώρων οἷα δίδωσι κακῶν, ἕτερος δὲ ἐάων....
ᾧ δέ κε τῶν λυγρῶν δώῃ, λωβητὸν ἔθηκε,
καί ἑ κακὴ βούβρωστις ἐπὶ χθόνα δῖαν ἐλαύνει,
φοιτᾷ δ' οὔτε θεοῖσι τετιμένος οὔτε βροτοῖσιν.

                              24.527–28, 531–33

24   Ὃν δ' αὖ δήμου τ' ἄνδρα ἴδοι βοόωντά τ' ἐφεύροι,
τὸν σκήπτρῳ ἐλάσασκεν ὁμοκλήσασκέ τε μύθῳ·
"Δαιμόνι', ἀτρέμας ἧσο καὶ ἄλλων μῦθον ἄκουε,

οἳ σέο φέρτεροί εἰσι, σὺ δ' ἀπτόλεμος καὶ ἄναλκις,
οὔτέ ποτ' ἐν πολέμῳ ἐναρίθμιος οὔτ' ἐνὶ βουλῇ.

2.198–202

25   πλῆξεν· ὁ δ' ἰδνώθη, θαλερὸν δέ οἱ ἔκπεσε δάκρυ·
σμῶδιξ δ' αἱματόεσσα μεταφρένου ἐξυπανέστη
σκήπτρου ὑπὸ χρυσέου· ὁ δ' ἄρ' ἕζετο τάρβησέν τε,
ἀλγήσας δ' ἀχρεῖον ἰδὼν ἀπομόρξατο δάκρυ·
οἱ δὲ καὶ ἀχνύμενοί περ ἐπ' αὐτῷ ἡδὺ γέλασσαν.

2.266–70

26   ... αὐτὰρ Ἀχιλλεὺς
δακρύσας ἑτάρων ἄφαρ ἕζετο νόσφι λιασθείς,
θῖν' ἐφ' ἁλὸς πολιῆς, ὁρόων ἐπὶ οἴνοπα πόντον.

1.348–50

27   ... ὄφρ' ἐὺ εἰδῇς
ὅσσον φέρτερός εἰμι σέθεν, στυγέῃ δὲ καὶ ἄλλος
ἶσον ἐμοὶ φάσθαι καὶ ὁμοιωθήμεναι ἄντην.

1.185–87

29   Ὣς ἔφαθ', οἱ δ' ἄρα πάντες ἀκὴν ἐγένοντο σιωπῇ·
αἴδεσθεν μὲν ἀνήνασθαι, δεῖσαν δ' ὑποδέχθαι.

7.92–93

30   Τρῶας δὲ τρόμος αἰνὸς ὑπήλυθε γυῖα ἕκαστον,
Ἕκτορί τ' αὐτῷ θυμὸς ἐνὶ στήθεσσι πάτασσεν·
ἀλλ' οὔ πως ἔτι εἶχεν ὑποτρέσαι οὐδ' ἀναδῦναι.

7.215–17

31   Ζεὺς δὲ πατὴρ Αἴανθ' ὑψίζυγος ἐν φόβον ὦρσε·
στῆ δὲ ταφών, ὄπιθεν δὲ σάκος βάλεν ἑπταβόειον,
τρέσσε δὲ παπτήνας ἐφ' ὁμίλου, θηρὶ ἐοικώς.

11.544–46

32   καὶ τότε δὴ χρύσεια πατὴρ ἐπίταινε τάλαντα·
ἐν δ' ἐτίθει δύο κῆρε τανηλεγέος θανάτοιο,

Τρώων θ᾽ ἱπποδάμων καὶ Ἀχαιῶν χαλκοχιτώνων,
ἕλκε δὲ μέσσα λαβών· ῥέπε δ᾽ αἴσιμον ἦμαρ Ἀχαιῶν.

8.69–72

33 ξυνὸς Ἐνυάλιος, καί τε κτανέοντα κατέκτα.

18.309

37 "Μήτ᾽ ἄρ τις νῦν κτήματ᾽ Ἀλεξάνδροιο δεχέσθω
μήθ᾽ Ἑλένην· γνωτὸν δὲ καὶ ὃς μάλα νήπιός ἐστιν,
ὡς ἤδη Τρώεσσιν ὀλέθρου πείρατ᾽ ἐφῆπται."
Ὣς ἔφαθ᾽, οἱ δ᾽ ἄρα πάντες ἐπίαχον υἷες Ἀχαιῶν.

7.400–3

39 Εὖ γὰρ ἐγὼ τόδε οἶδα κατὰ φρένα καὶ κατὰ θυμόν·
ἔσσεται ἦμαρ ὅτ᾽ ἄν ποτ᾽ ὀλώλῃ Ἴλιος ἱρὴ
καὶ Πρίαμος καὶ λαὸς ἐυμμελίω Πριάμοιο·
ἀλλ᾽ οὔ μοι Τρώων τόσσον μέλει ἄλγος ὀπίσσω,
οὔτ᾽ αὐτῆς Ἑκάβης οὔτε Πριάμοιο ἄνακτος
οὔτε κασιγνήτων, οἵ κεν πολέες τε καὶ ἐσθλοὶ
ἐν κονίῃσι πέσοιεν ὑπ᾽ ἀνδράσι δυσμενέεσσιν,
ὅσσον σεῖ᾽, ὅτε κέν τις Ἀχαιῶν χαλκοχιτώνων
δακρυόεσσαν ἄγηται, ἐλεύθερον ἦμαρ ἀπούρας ....
Ἀλλά με τεθνηῶτα χυτὴ κατὰ γαῖα καλύπτοι,
πρίν γέ τι σῆς τε βοῆς σοῦ θ᾽ ἑλκηθμοῖο πυθέσθαι.

6.447–55, 464–65

40 καίωμεν πυρὰ πολλά, σέλας δ᾽ εἰς οὐρανὸν ἵκῃ,
μή πως καὶ διὰ νύκτα κάρη κομόωντες Ἀχαιοὶ
φεύγειν ὁρμήσονται ἐπ᾽ εὐρέα νῶτα θαλάσσης ....
ἀλλ᾽ ὥς τις τούτων γε βέλος καὶ οἴκοθι πέσσῃ
   ... ἵνα τις στυγέῃσι καὶ ἄλλος
Τρωσὶν ἐφ᾽ ἱπποδάμοισι φέρειν πολύδακρυν Ἄρεα.

8.509–11, 513, 515–16

41 οἱ δ᾽ ἔτι κὰμ μέσσον πεδίον φοβέοντο βόες ὥς,
ἅς τε λέων ἐφόβησε μολὼν ἐν νυκτὸς ἀμολγῷ ....

ὡς τοὺς Ἀτρεΐδης ἔπεφε κρείων Ἀγαμέμνων,
αἰὲν ἀποκτείνων τὸν ὀπίστατον· οἱ δὲ φέβοντο.

11.172–73, 177–78

42   "Νῦν δ' ὅτε πέρ μοι ἔδωκε Κρόνου πάις ἀγκυλομήτεω
κῦδος ἀρέσθ' ἐπὶ νηυσί, θαλάσσῃ τ' ἔλσαι Ἀχαιούς,
νήπιε, μηκέτι ταῦτα νοήματα φαῖν' ἐνὶ δήμῳ·
οὐ γάρ τις Τρώων ἐπιπείσεται· οὐ γὰρ ἐάσω."...
Ὣς Ἕκτωρ ἀγόρευ', ἐπὶ δὲ Τρῶες κελάδησαν.

18.293–96, 310

43   Ὤ μοι ἐγών, εἰ μέν κε πύλας καὶ τείχεα δύω,
Πουλυδάμας μοι πρῶτος ἐλεγχείην ἀναθήσει ....
νῦν δ' ἐπεὶ ὤλεσα λαὸν ἀτασθαλίῃσιν ἐμῇσιν,
αἰδέομαι Τρῶας καὶ Τρῳάδας ἑλκεσιπέπλους,
μή ποτέ τις εἴπῃσι κακώτερος ἄλλος ἐμεῖο·
"'Ἕκτωρ ἦφι βίηφι πιθήσας ὤλεσε λαόν."...
Εἰ δέ κεν ἀσπίδα μὲν καταθείομαι ὀμφαλόεσσαν
καὶ κόρυθα βριαρήν, δόρυ δὲ πρὸς τεῖχος ἐρείσας
αὐτὸς ἰὼν Ἀχιλῆος ἀμύμονος ἀντίος ἔλθω ....
Ἀλλὰ τί ἤ μοι ταῦτα φίλος διελέξατο θυμός;
μή μιν ἐγὼ μὲν ἵκωμαι ἰών, ὁ δέ μ' οὐκ ἐλεήσει
οὐδέ τί μ' αἰδέσεται, κτενέει δέ με γυμνὸν ἐόντα
αὔτως ὥς τε γυναῖκα ....

22.99–100, 104–7, 111–13, 122–25

44   Ἕκτορα δ', ὡς ἐνόησεν, ἕλε τρόμος· οὐδ' ἄρ' ἔτ' ἔτλη
αὖθι μένειν,...
        ... οὐχ ἱερήιον οὐδὲ βοείην
ἀρνύσθην, ἅ τε ποσσὶν ἀέθλια γίνεται ἀνδρῶν,
ἀλλὰ πέρὶ ψυχῆς θέον Ἕκτορος ἱπποδάμοιο.

22.136–37, 159–61

45   Λίσσομ' ὑπὲρ ψυχῆς καὶ γούνων σῶν τε τοκήων ....

22.338

47   ἀλλ' ἕνα παῖδα τέκεν παναώριον· οὐδέ νυ τόν γε

γηράσκοντα κομίζω, ἐπεὶ μάλα τηλόθι πάτρης
ἧμαι ἐνὶ Τροίῃ, σέ τε κήδων ἠδὲ σὰ τέκνα.

24.540–42

48   Οὐ γὰρ ἐμοὶ ψυχῆς ἀντάξιον οὐδ' ὅσα φασὶν
Ἴλιον ἐκτῆσθαι, εὖ ναιόμενον πτολίεθρον ....
ληιστοὶ μὲν γάρ τε βόες καὶ ἴφια μῆλα ....
ἀνδρὸς δὲ ψυχὴ πάλιν ἐλθεῖν οὔτε λεϊστή.

9.401–2, 406, 408

49   ... ἄμμιν ... οἷσιν ἄρα Ζεὺς
ἐκ νεότητος ἔδωκε καὶ ἐς γῆρας τολυπεύειν
ἀργαλέους πολέμους, ὄφρα φθιόμεσθα ἕκαστος.

14.85–87

51   πῇ ἔβαν εὐχωλαί, ὅτε δὴ φάμεν εἶναι ἄριστοι,
ἃς ὁπότ' ἐν Λήμνῳ κενεαυχέες ἠγοράασθε,
ἔσθοντες κρέα πολλὰ βοῶν ὀρθοκραιράων,
πίνοντες κρητῆρας ἐπιστεφέας οἴνοιο,
Τρώων ἄνθ' ἑκατόν τε διηκοσίων τε ἕκαστος
στήσεσθ' ἐν πολέμῳ· νῦν δ' οὐδ' ἑνὸς ἄξιοί εἰμεν.

8.229–34

54   κὰδ' δέ κεν εὐχωλὴν Πριάμῳ καὶ Τρωσὶ λίποιεν
Ἀργείην Ἑλένην, ἧς εἵνεκα πολλοὶ Ἀχαιῶν
ἐν Τροίῃ ἀπόλοντο, φίλης ἀπὸ πατρίδος αἴης;...
Οὕτω δὴ μέμονας Τρώων πόλιν εὐρυάγυιαν
καλλείψειν, ἧς εἵνεκ' ὀιζύομεν κακὰ πολλα;

2.176–78, 14.88–89

55   Αὐτίκα τεθναίην, ἐπεὶ οὐκ ἄρ' ἔμελλον ἑταίρῳ
κτεινομένῳ ἐπαμῦναι· ὁ μὲν μάλα τηλόθι πάτρης
ἔφθιτ', ἐμεῖο δὲ δῆσεν ἀρῆς ἀλκτῆρα γενέσθαι....
νῦν δ' εἶμ', ὄφρα φίλης κεφαλῆς ὀλετῆρα κιχείω,
Ἕκτορα· κῆρα δ' ἐγὼ τότε δέξομαι, ὁππότε κεν δὴ
Ζεὺς ἐθέλῃ τελέσαι ἠδ' ἀθάνατοι θεοὶ ἄλλοι.

18.98–100, 114–16

56   εὖ νύ τοι οἶδα καὶ αὐτὸς ὅ μοι μόρος ἐνθάδ' ὀλέσθαι,
      νόσφι φίλου πατρὸς καὶ μητέρος· ἀλλὰ καὶ ἔμπης
      οὐ λήξω πρὶν Τρῶας ἄδην ἐλάσαι πολέμοιο.

                                          19.421–23

58   Γουνοῦμαι σ', Ἀχιλεῦ· σὺ δέ μ' αἴδεο καί μ' ἐλέησον·
      ἀντί τοί εἰμ' ἱκέταο, διοτρεφές, αἰδοίοιο·
      πὰρ γὰρ σοὶ πρώτῳ πασάμην Δημήτερος ἀκτήν,
      ἤματι τῷ ὅτε μ' εἷλες ἐυκτιμένῃ ἐν ἀλωῇ,
      καί μ' ἐπέρασσας ἄνευθεν ἄγων πατρός τε φίλων τε
      Λῆμνον ἐς ἠγαθέην, ἑκατόμβοιον δέ τοι ἦλφον.
      Νῦν δὲ λύμην τρὶς τόσσα πορών· ἠὼς δέ μοί ἐστιν
      ἥδε δυωδεκάτη, ὅτ' ἐς Ἴλιον εἰλήλουθα
      πολλὰ παθών· νῦν αὖ με τεῇς ἐν χερσὶν ἔθηκε
      μοῖρ' ὀλοή· μέλλω που ἀπεχθέσθαι Διὶ πατρί,
      ὅς με σοὶ αὖτις ἔδωκε· μινυνθάδιον δέ με μήτηρ
      γείνατο Λαοθόη, θυγάτηρ Ἄλταο γέροντος ....

                                          21.74–85

59   Ἀλλά, φίλος, θάνε καὶ σύ· τί ἦ ὀλοφύρεαι οὕτως;
      κάτθανε καὶ Πάτροκλος, ὅ περ σέο πολλὸν ἀμείνων·
      οὐχ ὁράᾳς οἷος καὶ ἐγὼ καλός τε μέγας τε;
      πατρὸς δ' εἴμ' ἀγαθοῖο, θεὰ δέ με γείνατο μήτηρ·
      ἀλλ' ἔπι τοι καὶ ἐμοὶ θάνατος καὶ μοῖρα κραταιή·
      ἔσσεται ἢ ἠὼς ἢ δείλη ἢ μέσον ἦμαρ,
      ὁππότε τις καὶ ἐμεῖο Ἄρῃ ἐκ θυμὸν ἕληται ....

                                          21.106–12

61   Αὐτὰρ ὅ γ' ὥς τε λέων ὀλοόφρων βουσὶν ἐπελθών,
      αἵ ῥά τ' ἐν εἰαμενῇ ἕλεος μεγάλοιο νέμονται
      μυρίαι ...,
      ... αἱ δέ τε πᾶσαι ὑπέτρεσαν· ὣς τότ' Ἀχαιοὶ
      θεσπεσίως ἐφόβηθεν ὑφ' Ἕκτορι καὶ Διὶ πατρὶ
      πάντες ....
      Ὡς δ' ὅτε πῦρ ἀίδηλον ἐν ἀξύλῳ ἐμπέσῃ ὕλῃ,
      πάντῃ τ' εἰλυφόων ἄνεμος φέρει, οἱ δέ τε θάμνοι
      πρόρριζοι πίπτουσιν ἐπειγόμενοι πυρὸς ὁρμῇ·

ὡς ἄρ' ὑπ' Ἀτρεΐδῃ Ἀγαμέμνονι πῖπτε κάρηνα
Τρώων φευγόντων ....

15.630–32, 636–38, 11.155–59

64 Τῷ νῦν σοὶ μὲν ἐγὼ ξεῖνος φίλος Ἄργεϊ μέσσῳ
εἰμί ....
ἔγχεα δ' ἀλλήλων ἀλεώμεθα καὶ δὶ ὁμίλου.

6.224–26

65 Τὸν δ' αὖτε προσέειπε Θέτις κατὰ δάκρυ χέουσα·
"Ὠκύμορος δή μοι, τέκος, ἔσσεαι, οἷ' ἀγορεύεις."

18.94–95

66 τρεῖς τε κασιγνήτους, τούς μοι μία γείνατο μήτηρ,
κηδείους ....

19.293–94

67   ... ἐμοὶ δέ κε κέρδιον εἴη
σεῦ ἀφαμαρτούσῃ χθόνα δύμεναι· οὐ γὰρ ἔτ' ἄλλη
ἔσται θαλπωρή, ἐπεὶ ἂν σύ γε πότμον ἐπίσπῃς,
ἀλλ' ἄχε' ....

6.410–13

68 Ἄνερ, ἀπ' αἰῶνος νέος ὤλεο, κὰδ δέ με χήρην
λείπεις ἐν μεγάροισι· πάις δ' ἔτι νήπιος αὔτως,
ὃν τέκομεν σύ τ' ἐγώ τε δυσάμμοροι, οὐδέ μιν οἴω
ἥβην ἵξεσθαι ....
οὐ γάρ μοι θνήσκων λεχέων ἐκ χεῖρας ὄρεξας,
οὐδέ τί μοι εἶπες πυκινὸν ἔπος, οὔ τέ κεν αἰεὶ
μεμνήμην νύκτάς τε καὶ ἤματα δάκρυ χέουσα.

24.725–28, 743–45

69   ... αὐτὰρ Ἀχιλλεὺς
κλαῖε φίλου ἑτάρου μεμνημένος, οὐδέ μιν ὕπνος
ᾕρει πανδαμάτωρ, ἀλλ' ἐστρέφετ' ἔνθα καὶ ἔνθα ....

24.3–5

70   Αὐτὰρ ἐπεὶ πόσιος καὶ ἐδητύος ἐξ ἔρον ἕντο,
     ἤτοι Δαρδανίδης Πρίαμος θαύμαζ' Ἀχιλῆα,
     ὅσσος ἔην οἷός τε· θεοῖσι γὰρ ἄντα ἐῴκει·
     αὐτὰρ ὁ Δαρδανίδην Πρίαμον θαύμαζεν Ἀχιλλεύς,
     εἰσορόων ὄψιν τ' ἀγαθὴν καὶ μῦθον ἀκούων.
     Αὐτὰρ ἐπεὶ τάρπησαν ἐς ἀλλήλους ὁρόωντες ....
                                                24.628–33

72   Ὣς ὁ μὲν αὖθι πεσὼν κοιμήσατο χάλκεον ὕπνον
     οἰκτρός, ἀπὸ μνηστῆς ἀλόχου, ἀστοῖσιν ἀρήγων ....
                                                11.241–42

73   ἕνδεκα δ' ἤματα θυμὸν ἐτέρπετο οἷσι φίλοισιν
     ἐλθὼν ἐκ Λήμνοιο· δυωδεκάτῃ δέ μιν αὖτις
     χερσὶν Ἀχιλλῆος θεὸς ἔμβαλεν, ὅς μιν ἔμελλε
     πέμψειν εἰς Ἀΐδαο καὶ οὐκ ἐθέλοντα νέεσθαι.
                                                21.45–48

74   αἵματί οἱ δεύοντο κόμαι Χαρίτεσσιν ὁμοῖαι ....
                                                17.51

75   ... ἔχες δ' ἀλόχους κεδνὰς καὶ νήπια τέκνα.
                                                24.730

     Ἔνθα δ' ἐπ' αὐτάων πλυνοὶ εὐρέες ἐγγὺς ἔασι
     καλοὶ λαΐνεοι, ὅθι εἵματα σιγαλόεντα
     πλύνεσκον Τρώων ἄλοχοι καλαί τε θύγατρες
     τὸ πρὶν ἐπ' εἰρήνης, πρὶν ἐλθεῖν υἷας Ἀχαιῶν·
     τῇ ῥα παραδραμέτην, φεύγων, ὁ δ' ὄπισθε διώκων.
                                                22.153–57

77   Ὄφρα μὲν ἠὼς ἦν καὶ ἀέξετο ἱερὸν ἦμαρ,
     τόφρα μάλ' ἀμφοτέρων βέλε' ἥπτετο, πῖπτε δὲ λαός·
     ἦμος δὲ δρυτόμος περ ἀνὴρ ὡπλίσσατο δεῖπνον
     οὔρεος ἐν βήσσῃσιν, ἐπεί τε ἐκορέσσατο χεῖρας
     τάμνων δένδρεα μακρά, ἄδος τέ μιν ἵκετο θυμόν,

σίτου τε γλυκεροῖο περὶ φρένας ἵμερος αἱρεῖ,
τῆμος σφῇ ἀρετῇ Δαναοὶ ῥήξαντο φάλαγγας.

11.84–90

78   ἐκ δὲ τίναχθεν ὀδόντες, ἐνέπλησθεν δέ οἱ ἄμφω
αἵματος ὀφθαλμοί· τὸ δ' ἀνὰ στόμα καὶ κατὰ ῥῖνας
πρῆσε χανών. θανάτου δὲ μέλαν νέφος ἀμφεκάλυψεν.

16.348–50

Bibliography

Africa, Thomas W. (1974). *The Immense Majesty: A History of Rome and the Roman Empire*. New York: Crowell.

Austin, Norman (1994). *Helen of Troy and Her Shameless Phantom*. Ithaca: Cornell Univ. Press.

Autran, Charles (1938–39–44). *Homère et les origines sacerdotales de l'épopée grecque*. 3 vols. Paris: Denoël.

Berlin, Isaiah (1980). "Benjamin Disraeli, Karl Marx and the Search for Identity." In *Against the Current: Essays in the History of Ideas*. Ed. H. Hardy. New York: Viking. [Orig. in *Transactions of the Jewish Historical Society of England* 22 (1968–69).]

Blum, Lawrence A., and Victor J. Seidler (1989). *A Truer Liberty: Simone Weil and Marxism*. New York: Routledge.

Booth, Wayne C. (1988). *The Company We Keep: An Ethics of Fiction*. Berkeley: Univ. of California Press.

Caputo, Philip (1977). *A Rumor of War*. New York: Ballantine [1978 rpt.].

Clarke, Howard (1981). *Homer's Readers: A Historical Introduction to the Iliad and the Odyssey*. Newark: Univ. of Delaware Press.

Clarke, Michael (1995). "Between Lions and Men: Images of the Hero in the *Iliad*." *Greek, Roman, and Byzantine Studies* 36:137–60.

Coles, Robert (1987). *Simone Weil: A Modern Pilgrimage*. Reading, MA: Addison-Wesley.

Cook, Bradford (1953). "Simone Weil: Art and the Artist under God." *Yale French Studies* 12:73–80.

Crotty, Kevin (1994). *The Poetics of Supplication: Homer's Iliad and Odyssey*. Ithaca: Cornell Univ. Press.

Cruise, P.E. (1986). "The Problem of Being Simone Weil." *Judaism* 35:98–106.

Dunaway, John M. (1984). *Simone Weil*. Boston: Twayne.

Edwards, Mark W. (1987). *Homer: Poet of the Iliad*. Baltimore: Johns Hopkins Univ. Press.

———. (1991). *The Iliad: A Commentary*. Vol. 5: *Books 17–20*. Cambridge: Cambridge Univ. Press.

Edwards, Thomas R. (1971). "Epic and the Modern Reader: A Note on Simone Weil." In *Imagination and Power*. London: Chatto & Windus. Pp. 10–16.

Evelyn-White, H.G., ed. and trans. (1936). *Hesiod, the Homeric Hymns and Homerica*. Cambridge: Harvard Univ. Press.

Ferber, Michael K. (1981). "Simone Weil's *Iliad*." In White (1981) 63–86.

Fiedler, Leslie (1972). "Simone Weil: Prophet out of Israel, Saint of the Absurd." In *To the Gentiles*. New York: Stein and Day. Pp. 5–30. [Orig.: *Commentary* (Jan 1951) 36–46.]

Fiori, Gabriella (1989). *Simone Weil: An Intellectual Biography*. Trans. J.R. Berrigan. Athens: Univ. of Georgia Press. [Orig.: *Simone Weil: biografia di un pensiero*. Milan: Garzanti, 1981.]

Fraisse, Simone (1978). "Simone Weil et le monde antique." In Kahn (1978) 193–201.

Fränkel, Hermann (1997). "Essence and Nature of the Homeric Similes." In Wright and Jones (1997) 103–23. [Orig. in *Die homerischen Gleichnisse*. Göttingen: Vandenhoeck & Ruprecht, 1921. Pp. 98–114.]

Frye, Northrop (1957). *Anatomy of Criticism: Four Essays*. Princeton: Princeton Univ. Press.

Fussell, Paul (1975). *The Great War and Modern Memory*. Oxford: Oxford Univ. Press.

———. (1989). *Wartime: Understanding and Behavior in the Second World War*. Oxford: Oxford Univ. Press.

Gaillardot, Jacqueline (1982). "L'*Iliade*: Poème de la force?" *Cahiers Simone Weil* 5:184–91.

Garraty, John A., and Peter Gay, eds. (1972). *The Columbia History of the World*. New York: Harper and Row.

Giniewski, Paul (1978). *Simone Weil, ou la haine de soi*. Paris: Berg International.

Gladden, E. Norman (1967). *Ypres, 1917: A Personal Account*. London: Kimber.

Gottschall, Jonathan (2001). "Homer's Human Animal: Ritual Combat in the *Iliad*." *Philosophy and Literature* 25:278–94.

Gould, J.P. (1973). "Hiketeia." *Journal of Hellenic Studies* 93:74–103.

Gray, Francine du Plessix (2001). *Simone Weil*. New York: Viking.

Griffin, Jasper (1980). *Homer on Life and Death*. Oxford: Clarendon Press.

Hainsworth, Bryan (1993). *The Iliad: A Commentary*. Vol. 3: *Books 9–12*. Cambridge: Cambridge Univ. Press.

Heiden, Bruce (1998). "The Simile of the Fugitive Homicide, *Iliad* 24.480–84: Analogy, Foiling, and Allusion." *American Journal of Philology* 119:1–10.

Holoka, James P. (1991). "Homer, Oral Poetry Theory, and Comparative Literature: Major Trends and Controversies in Twentieth-Century Criticism." In *Zweihundert Jahre Homer-Forschung: Rückblick und Ausblick*. Ed. J. Latacz. Stuttgart and Leipzig: Teubner. Pp. 456–81.

Hourdin, Georges (1989). *Simone Weil*. Paris: La Découverte.

Janko, Richard (1992). *The Iliad: A Commentary*. Vol. 4: *Books 13–16*. Cambridge: Cambridge Univ. Press.

Kahn, Gilbert, ed. (1978). *Simone Weil: philosophe, historienne et mystique*. Paris: Aubier Montaigne.

Kakridis, Johannes T. (1949). *Homeric Researches*. Lund: Gleerup. Rpt. New York: Garland, 1987.

Kaufmann, Walter, trans. (1954). *The Portable Nietzsche*. New York: Viking.

Kirk, G.S. (1985). *The Iliad: A Commentary*. Vol. 1: *Books 1–4*. Cambridge: Cambridge Univ. Press.

———. (1990). *The Iliad: A Commentary*. Vol. 2: *Books 5–8*. Cambridge: Cambridge Univ. Press.

Knauer, Georg N. (1979). *Die Aeneis und Homer*. 2nd ed. Göttingen: Vandenhoeck und Ruprecht.

Knopp, Josephine Z. (1984). "The Carnal God: Simone Weil's Anti-Judaic Perspective." *Mysticism, Nihilism, Feminism: New Critical Essays on the Theology of Simone Weil*. Ed. T.A. Idinopulos and J.Z. Knopp. Johnson City, TN: Institute for Social Sciences and Arts. Pp. 117–38.

Knox, Bernard M.W. (1989). "The Spanish Tragedy." In *Essays Ancient and Modern*. Baltimore: Johns Hopkins Univ. Press. [Orig. in *New York Review of Books* (26 March 1987).]

———. (1990). "Introduction." In *Homer: The Iliad*. Trans. R. Fagles. New York: Viking. Pp. 1–64.

———. (1994). "Godlike Achilles." In *Backing into the Future: The Classical Tradition and Its Renewal*. New York: Norton. Pp. 19–47.

Latacz, Joachim (1996). *Homer: His Art and His World*. Trans. J.P. Holoka. Ann Arbor: Univ. of Michigan Press.

———. (2001). *Troia und Homer: Der Weg zur Lösung eines alten Rätsels*. Munich/Berlin: Koehler & Amelang.

———, ed. (1991). *Homer: Die Dichtung und ihre Deutung*. Darmstadt: Wissenschaftliche Buchgesellschaft.

Latacz, Joachim, et al. (2000). *Homers Ilias: Gesamtkommentar*. Vol. 1.2. Munich/Leipzig: Saur.

Lateiner, Donald (1995). *Sardonic Smile: Nonverbal Behavior in Homeric Epic*. Ann Arbor: Univ. of Michigan Press.

Lattimore, Richmond, trans. (1951). *The Iliad of Homer*. Chicago: Univ. of Chicago Press.

Lee, D.J.N. (1964). *The Similes of the Iliad and the Odyssey Compared*. Melbourne: Melbourne Univ. Press.

Little, J.P. (1973). *Simone Weil: A Bibliography*. London: Grant and Cutler.

———. (1988). *Simone Weil: Waiting on the Truth*. Oxford: Berg.

Lloyd-Jones, Hugh (1961). "Greek Studies in Modern Oxford" [Oxford Inaugural Lecture]. Rpt. in *Blood for the Ghosts: Classical Influences in the Nineteenth and Twentieth Centuries*. Baltimore: Johns Hopkins Univ. Press, 1982. Pp. 13–31.

———, trans. (1979). *Aeschylus, Oresteia: Agamemnon*. London: Duckworth.

Mack Smith, Denis (1976). *Mussolini's Roman Empire*. New York: Viking.

Mackie, Hilary (1996). *Talking Trojan: Speech and Community in the Iliad*. Lanham, MD: Rowman & Littlefield.

Macleod, Colin W., ed. (1982). *Homer: Iliad, Book XXIV*. Cambridge: Cambridge Univ. Press.

Maude, L. and A., trans. (1933). *War and Peace: A Novel by Leo Tolstoy*. Rev. ed. London: Oxford Univ. Press.

McAuslan, Ian, and Peter Walcot, eds. (1998). *Greece and Rome Studies: Homer.* Oxford: Oxford Univ. Press, 1998.

McLane-Iles, Betty (1987). *Uprooting and Integration in the Writings of Simone Weil.* New York: Peter Lang.

McLellan, David (1989). *Simone Weil: Utopian Pessimist.* London: Macmillan.

Mueller, Martin (1984). *The Iliad.* London: Allen & Unwin.

Murray, Gilbert (1934). *The Rise of the Greek Epic.* 4th ed. Oxford: Oxford Univ. Press.

Nevin, Thomas R. (1991). *Simone Weil: Portrait of a Self-Exiled Jew.* Chapel Hill: Univ. of North Carolina Press.

Nimis, Stephen A. (1987). *Narrative Semiotics in the Epic Tradition: The Simile.* Bloomington: Indiana Univ. Press.

O'Brien, Tim (1990). *The Things They Carried.* Boston: Houghton Mifflin.

Owen, E.T. (1946). *The Story of the Iliad as Told in the Iliad.* Toronto: Clarke, Irwin. Rpt. Wauconda, IL: Bolchazy-Carducci, 1989.

Parry, Adam (1963). "The Two Voices of Virgil's *Aeneid.*" *Arion* 2.4:66–80. Rpt. in *Virgil: A Collection of Critical Essays.* Ed. S. Commager. Englewood Cliffs, NJ: Prentice-Hall, 1966. Pp. 107–23.

Pedrick, Victoria (1982). "Supplication in the *Iliad* and the *Odyssey.*" *Transactions of the American Philological Association* 112:125–40.

Pétrement, Simone (1976). *Simone Weil: A Life.* Trans. R. Rosenthal. New York: Pantheon. [Orig.: *La Vie de Simone Weil.* 2 vols. Paris: Fayard, 1973.]

Poole, Adrian (1992). "War and Grace: The Force of Simone Weil on Homer." *Arion* 2.1:1–15.

Postlethwaite, Norman (1988). "Thersites in the *Iliad.*" *Greece and Rome* 35:123–36. Rpt. in McAuslan and Walcot (1998) 83–95.

———. (2000). *Homer's Iliad: A Commentary on the Translation of Richmond Lattimore.* Exeter: Univ. of Exeter Press.

Pulleyn, Simon, ed. and trans. (2000). *Homer: Iliad Book One.* Oxford: Oxford Univ. Press.

Putnam, Michael C.J. (1965). *The Poetry of the Aeneid: Four Studies in Imaginative Unity and Design.* Cambridge: Harvard Univ. Press.

Redfield, James M. (1975). *Nature and Culture in the Iliad: The Tragedy of Hector.* Chicago: Univ. of Chicago Press.

Remarque, Erich Maria (1929). *All Quiet on the Western Front.* Trans. A.W. Wheen. New York: Fawcett [1964]. [Orig.: *Im Westen Nichts Neues.* Berlin: Propylaen-Verlag, 1929.]

The Revised English Bible with the Apocrypha (1989). Oxford: Oxford Univ. Press; Cambridge: Cambridge Univ. Press.

Richardson, Nicholas (1993). *The Iliad: A Commentary.* Vol. 6: *Books 21–24.* Cambridge: Cambridge Univ. Press.

Rosen, Fred (1979). "Marxism, Mysticism, and Liberty: The Influence of Simone Weil on Albert Camus." *Political Theory* 7:301–19.

Russell, Bertrand (1969). *The Autobiography of Bertrand Russell: 1944-1969.* New York: Simon and Schuster.

Schadewaldt, Wolfgang (1997a). "Hector and Andromache." In Wright and Jones (1997) 124–42. [Orig. in *Von Homers Welt und Werk*. 3rd ed. Stuttgart: Koehler Verlag, 1959. Pp. 207–29.]

———. (1997b). "Achilles' Decision." In Wright and Jones (1997) 143–69. [Orig. in *Von Homers Welt und Werk*. 3rd ed. Stuttgart: Koehler Verlag, 1959. Pp. 234–67.]

Schein, Seth L. (1984). *The Mortal Hero: An Introduction to Homer's Iliad*. Berkeley: Univ. of California Press.

Segal, Charles P. (1971). *The Theme of the Mutilation of the Corpse in the Iliad*. Leiden: Brill.

Shay, Jonathan (1994). *Achilles in Vietnam: Combat Trauma and the Undoing of Character*. New York: Atheneum.

Sheppard, J.T. (1922). *The Pattern of the Iliad*. London: Methuen.

Simonsuuri, Kirsti (1985). "Simone Weil's Interpretation of Homer." *French Studies* 39:166–77.

Steiner, George (1969). *Language and Silence*. Harmondsworth: Penguin.

———. (1993). "Sainte Simone: The Jewish Bases of Simone Weil's *via negativa* to the Philosophic Peaks." *Times Literary Supplement* (4 June): 3–4.

Summers, Joseph H. (1981). "Notes on Simone Weil's *Iliad*." In White (1981) 87–94

Syme, Ronald (1939). *The Roman Revolution*. Oxford: Clarendon Press.

Taplin, Oliver (1980). "The Shield of Achilles within the *Iliad*." *Greece and Rome* 27:1–21. Rpt. in Latacz (1991) 227-53 and McAuslan and Walcot (1998) 96–115.

Thompson, J.M. (1951). *Napoleon Bonaparte: His Rise and Fall*. New York: Oxford Univ. Press.

Van Herik, J. (1985). "Simone Weil's Religious Imagery: How Looking Becomes Eating." In *Immaculate and Powerful: The Female in Sacred Image and Social Reality*. Ed. C.W. Atkinson et al. Boston: Beacon. Pp. 260–82.

Weil, Simone (1951). *Waiting for God*. Trans. E. Craufurd. New York: Putnam. [Orig.: *Attente de Dieu*. Paris: La Colombe, 1950.]

———. (1952a). *Gravity and Grace*. Trans. E. Craufurd. London: Routledge. [Orig.: *La Pesanteur et la grâce*. Paris: Plon, 1947.]

———. (1952b). *The Need for Roots: Prelude to a Declaration of Duties towards Mankind*. Trans. A.F. Wills. Pref. T.S. Eliot. London: Routledge. [Orig.: *L'Enracinement: Prélude à une déclaration des devoirs envers l'être humain*. Paris: Gallimard, 1949; 2nd ed. 1952.]

———. (1953). *La Source grecque*. Paris: Gallimard.

———. (1956a). *The Iliad, or the Poem of Force*. Trans. M. McCarthy. Wallingford, PA: Pendle Hill.

———. (1956b). *The Notebooks of Simone Weil*. Trans. A. Wills. 2 vols. London: Routledge. [Orig.: *Les Cahiers de Simone Weil*. 3 vols. Paris: Plon, 1951-53–56.]

———. (1957). *Intimations of Christianity among the Ancient Greeks*. Ed. and trans. E.C. Geissbuhler. London: Routledge.

————. (1962a). *Selected Essays: 1934–1943*. Ed. R. Rees. London: Oxford Univ. Press.

————. (1962b). "The Power of Words." In Weil (1962a) 154–71, as rpt. in Weil (1977) 268–85. [Orig. "Ne recommençons pas la guerre de Troie." *Les Nouveaux Cahiers* (1, 15 April 1937): 8–10, 15–19.]

————. (1965). *Seventy Letters*. Trans. R. Rees. London: Oxford Univ. Press.

————. (1968). *On Science, Necessity, and the Love of God*. Ed. and trans. R. Rees. London: Oxford Univ. Press.

————. (1970). *First and Last Notebooks*. Trans. R. Rees. London: Oxford Univ. Press.

————. (1973a). *Oppression and Liberty*. Trans. A. Wills and J. Petrie. Amherst: Univ. of Massachusetts Press. [Orig. *Oppression et liberté*. Paris: Gallimard, 1955.]

————. (1973b). "Analysis of Oppression." In Weil (1973a) 56–83, as rpt. in Weil (1977) 126–52.

————. (1977). *The Simone Weil Reader*. Ed. G.A. Panichas. New York: McKay.

————. (1987). *Formative Writings: 1929–1941*. Ed. and trans. D.T. McFarland and W. van Ness. Amherst: Univ. of Massachusetts Press.

————. (1989). *Œuvres complètes*. Ed. A.A. Devaux and F. de Lussy. Vol. 2.3: *Écrits historiques et politiques: Vers la guerre (1937–1940)*. Ed. S. Fraisse. Paris: Gallimard.

White, George A., ed. (1981). *Simone Weil: Interpretations of a Life*. Amherst: Univ. of Massachusetts Press.

Wilamowitz-Moellendorff, Ulrich von, ed. (1969). *Euripides: Herakles*. Vol. 1. 3rd ed. [1st 1889.] Darmstadt: Wissenschaftliche Buchgesellschaft.

Willcock, Malcolm M. (1976). *A Companion to the Iliad, Based on the Translation by Richmond Lattimore*. Chicago: Univ. of Chicago Press.

Wilson, Christopher H., ed. and trans. (1996). *Homer: Iliad Books VIII and IX*. Warminster: Aris & Phillips.

Winch, Peter (1989). *Simone Weil: "The Just Balance."* Cambridge: Cambridge Univ. Press.

Wright, G.M., and P.V. Jones, trans. (1997). *Homer: German Scholarship in Translation*. Oxford: Clarendon Press.

Zanker, Graham (1994). *The Heart of Achilles: Characterization and Personal Ethics in the Iliad*. Ann Arbor: Univ. of Michigan Press.

Index Locorum

General Index